D1335773

01123

For Claudia Kemp H.O.
For Jenny, Colin and baby Kirsten M.R.

MYRIAD BOOKS LIMITED
35 Bishopsthorpe Road, London SE26 4PA

First published in 1992 by
FRANCES LINCOLN LIMITED
4 Torriano Mews
Torriano Avenue
London NW5 2RZ

ISBN 1 84746 048 8
EAN 9 781 84746 048 6

Printed in China

MINE!

Hiawyn Oram

Illustrated by
Mary Rees

MYRIAD BOOKS LIMITED

Isabel went to play with Claudia.
She climbed onto Claudia's rocking horse.

"Mine!" shrieked Claudia and pushed her off.

Isabel picked up Claudia's Carrot Top doll.

"Mine!" screamed Claudia and snatched
it away.

Isabel saw Claudia's wooden animals
piled up in an old shoebox. She took them
out and set them up on the carpet.

"No, no, no!" cried Claudia. "My moo cows.
My baa lambs!"

Claudia's mother put on their hats and
coats and gloves and scarves.
"What we need is some fresh air," she said.

Isabel and Claudia and Claudia's mother walked to the park. Claudia's mother pushed Claudia's new tricycle.

When they got to the park Isabel climbed
onto the tricycle.

"No no no!" yelled Claudia. "My bike,
my bike. Me! Me! Me!"
She pulled Isabel off the tricycle.

"Now Claudia, let Izzie have a turn,"
said Claudia's mother.
"No Izzie, no Izzie," screamed Claudia.

"Mine! Mine! Mine!" And she pushed
the tricycle out of Isabel's reach.
It ran down the hill.
          It ran faster and faster.
                    It rolled over and over.

They watched the bell fly off
and land in a bird's nest.

They watched the handlebars fly off
and land in a tree.

They watched the saddle fly off and land
in the bandstand and the saddlebag land
in a baby's pram.

They watched the wheels come off
and roll, one by one, into the road,
into the pond,

and into the park-keeper's hut.

They watched nuts and bolts and screws and chains spray into the air and across the grass and disappear forever into piles of leaves.

They ran down the hill

and stood staring at the battered broken
new tricycle frame . . .

"Yours," said Isabel
and went to feed the ducks.

RISING STARS
Mathematics

Year 2

Concept developed by
Cherri Moseley and Caroline Clissold

Year 2 Author Team
Belle Cottingham, Emma Low,
Cherri Moseley

The Publishers would like to thank the following for permission to reproduce copyright material.

Photo credits

Pages 10-11: calendar – George Ruiz via Flickr (https://creativecommons.org/licenses/by/2.0/); dartboard – SEEDLING/Shutterstock; runner and timer – wavebreakmedia/ Shutterstock; children – ArtisticCaptures/iStock; pages 24-5: pencils – S McTeir; snakes and ladders board – S McTeir; sweets – demc7/iStock; dice – charnsitr/Shutterstock; tile – carlos castilla/Shutterstock; ruler – ScofieldZa/Shutterstock; p37: dartboard – Boltenkoff/Shutterstock; pages 38-9: stationery – S McTeir; building (top) – Christian Mueller/Shutterstock; building (bottom) – ArTono/Shutterstock; sea urchin – Stephen Rees/Shutterstock; butterfly – MindStorm/Shutterstock; page 49: diamond – AnatolyM/ iStock; pages 50-1: 2p, 5p, 20p and 50p coins: claudiodivizia/iStock; 10p coin – S McTier; scales – Dori Oconnell/iStock; parcel – Marek Mnich/iStock; cakes – S McTeir; park – SolStock/iStock; clock – Dmitry Sheremeta/ Shutterstock; fish tank – energy/iStock; pages 62-3: coins – S McTeir; vending machine – Ben Harding/iStock; money box – S McTeir; cash machine – sanjagrujic/Shutterstock; fete stall – anthonyjhall/iStock; page 75: coins – Royal Mint; pages 76-7: whiteboard – piotr_pabijan/Shutterstock; tea bags – inthevisual/iStock; front door – 1Photodiva/iStock; piles of coins – S McTeir; jug and tumblers – S McTeir; page 87: - elderly crossing sign – PeterEtchells/iStock; phone – ET-ARTWORKS/iStock; gender sign – PiLens/Shutterstock; frog warning sign – manwolste/iStock; pages 88-9: child – Rob Mattingley/iStock (left); johavel/iStock (centre); nicolesy/iStock (right); cakes in tins – Shaiith/Shutterstock; clock – JoseGirate/iStock; calculator – maerapaso/iStock; page 101: Plimpton 322 – Wiki/PD; pages 102-3: clock tower – Paul Velgos/Shutterstock; thermometer – cumroeng chinnapan; mushroom pizza – kgfto/iStock; other pizzas – Maica/iStock; sweets – Vorobyeva/Shutterstock; fraction plate – Wikimedia Commons; pages 116-17: coins – S McTeir; bananas – peanut8481/Shutterstock; oranges – OLEKSANDR PEREPEPELYTSIA/iStock; apples – Akira3288/Shutterstock; tennis balls – Mihail Glushkov/iStock (also on page 127); coloured pencils – Ralf Neumann/Shutterstock (left); villorejo/iStock (right); fairy lights – adlifemarketing/iStock; pages 128-9: rabbit hutch – RachelKathrynGiles/iStock; Louvre Museum – Tania Zbrodko/Shutterstock; girl with pineapple – naluwan/Shutterstock; nursery school – Vereshchagin/Shutterstock; toy train – ivanastar/Shutterstock; metal robot - N center/Shutterstock; page 137: watermelon – adventtr/iStock; pages 138-9: pizza – Maica/iStock (left); karardaev/iStock (right); bottle of juice – S McTeir; analogue clock – mict/iStock; train – Catwalk Photos/ Shutterstock; page 149: children baking – Ms Jane Campbell/Shutterstock; pages 150-1: paint tins – Brooke Becker/Shutterstock; book – S McTeir; scoreboard – NoDerog/iStock; dog – Erik Lam/Shutterstock; bag – Carles Navarro/Shutterstock; packet – Pack/Shutterstock; ice-lolly – lucilang/iStock; ice-cream cone – subjug/iStock; pages 164-5: children on tricycles – perkmeup/ Shutterstock (top left); Chepko Danil Vitalevich/Shutterstock (top right); VikaRayu/Shutterstock (bottom left); HomeArt/Shutterstock (bottom right); sandwich – S McTeir; packs of pens – S McTeir; watch – S McTeir; word clock – Doug Jackson, DougsWordClocks.com; Prague Astronomical Clock – Steve Collis via Wikipedia Commons (CC by 2.0); pages 176-7: children – S McTeir; road sign – Butterfly Hunter/Shutterstock; child with bottle – Serhiy Kobyakov/Shutterstock; baby turtle – Kristina Ethridge/Shutterstock; wind farm – Andrey Yurlov/Shutterstock; page 187: map – nerucci/Shutterstock.

Acknowledgements

The reasoning skills on page 8 are based on John Mason's work on mathematical powers. See Mason, J. and Johnston-Wilder, S. (Eds.) (2004). Learners powers. *Fundamental constructs in Mathematics Education*. London: Routledge Falmer. 115-142.

ISBN: 978 1 78339 523 1

Text, design and layout © Rising Stars UK Ltd 2016

First published in 2016 by

Rising Stars UK Ltd, part of Hodder Education,

An Hachette UK Company

Carmelite House

50 Victoria Embankment

London EC4Y 0DZ

www.risingstars-uk.com

Authors: Belle Cottingham, Emma Low, Cherri Moseley

Programme consultants: Cherri Moseley, Caroline Clissold, Paul Broadbent

Publishers: Fiona Lazenby and Alexandra Riley

Editorial: Kate Baxter, Jane Carr, Sarah Chappelow, Jan Fisher, Lucy Hyde, Jackie Mace, Jane Morgan, Christine Vaughan, Sara Wiegand

Project manager: Sue Walton

Series and character design: Steve Evans

Illustrations by Steve Evans

Cover design: Steve Evans and Words & Pictures

Printed by Liberduplex, Barcelona

A catalogue record for this title is available from the British Library.

Contents

Introduction

Hello, I'm Lili. Welcome to *Rising Stars Mathematics!*

Look at the pictures at the beginning of the unit. Think about the mathematics you can see in the world around you.

Talk about the questions with your friends. Do you agree on the answers?

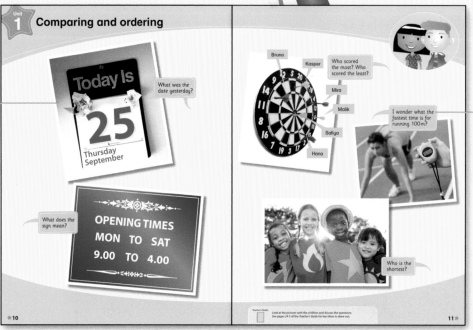

Read what Lili and Seb say. Can you spot if they have made a mistake?

Read the text and look at the diagrams to learn new maths skills. Your teacher will explain them.

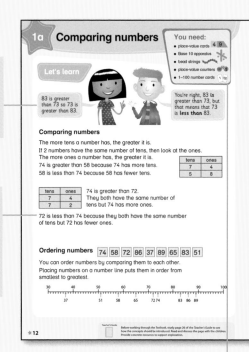

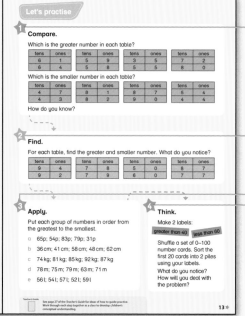

Do these activities to practise what you have learnt. Write the answers in your exercise book.

These questions will help you explore and investigate maths. You will need to think about them carefully.

Use these items to help you. Make sure you have everything you need.

And I'm Seb. We'll help you as you learn with this book!

Play the game at the end of the unit to practise what you have learnt.

Climb the ladder

Game board 1

Let's play

100

100

0

0

You need:
- place-value cards 4 9
- small pieces of card or paper
- 2 large envelopes or bags
- digit cards 0–9 0 9

Make sure you have everything you need.

1 Place-value ladder
Take turns to make a 2-digit number using place-value cards and place it, in the correct order, on the ladder.

2 Digit ladder
Take turns to make a 2-digit number using digit cards and place it, in the correct order, on the ladder.

3 Your ladder
Design your own game. Explain the rules and play with a partner.

Follow the instructions to use the gameboard in different ways.

See pages 34–5 of the Teacher's Guide. Explain the rules for each game and allow children to choose which to play. Encourage them to challenge themselves and practise what they have learnt in the unit.

Teacher's Guide

☆20

21☆

Try these activities to check what you have learnt in the unit. Have you understood all the new maths concepts?

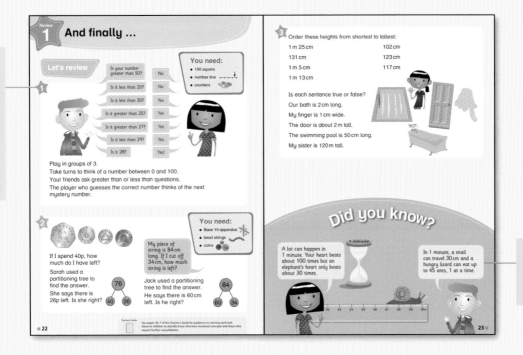

And finally ...

Review 1

Let's review

Is your number greater than 50?	No
Is it less than 20?	No
Is it less than 30?	Yes
Is it greater than 25?	Yes
Is it greater than 27?	Yes
Is it less than 29?	Yes
Is it 28?	Yes!

You need:
- 100 square
- number line
- counters

1
Play in groups of 3.
Take turns to think of a number between 0 and 100.
Your friends ask greater than or less than questions.
The player who guesses the correct number thinks of the next mystery number.

2
If I spend 40p, how much do I have left?
Sarah used a partitioning tree to find the answer.
She says there is 26p left. Is she right?
76 / 40 26

My piece of string is 84 cm long. If I cut off 34 cm, how much string is left?
Jack used a partitioning tree to find the answer.
He says there is 60 cm left. Is he right?
84 / 60 34

You need:
- Base 10 apparatus
- bead strings
- coins

3
Order these heights from shortest to tallest:

1 m 25 cm	102 cm
131 cm	123 cm
1 m 5 cm	117 cm
1 m 13 cm	

Is each sentence true or false?
Our bath is 2 cm long.
My finger is 1 cm wide.
The door is about 2 m tall.
The swimming pool is 50 cm long.
My sister is 120 m tall.

Did you know?

A lot can happen in 1 minute. Your heart beats about 100 times but an elephant's heart only beats about 30 times.

In 1 minute, a snail can travel 30 cm and a hungry lizard can eat up to 45 ants, 1 at a time.

Find out more about maths by reading these fun facts!

See pages 36–7 of the Teacher's Guide for guidance on running each task. Observe children to identify those who have mastered concepts and those who require further consolidation.

Teacher's Guide

☆22

23☆

Problem solving and reasoning

Try these ideas to develop your reasoning skills. Doing this will help you improve your mathematical thinking.

Make statements
Can you say what you notice about why something happens?

Convince
Can you persuade other people that your statements are correct?

Organise
Can you put things into groups, an order or a pattern?

Generalise
Can you make connections to describe rules and patterns?

Classify
Can you identify and name the groups you have organised things into?

Find examples
Can you give specific examples to fit a pattern or rule?

Imagine
Can you think of different ideas or ways to do things?

Explain
Can you explain your thinking and reasoning about a problem?

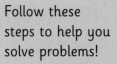
Follow these steps to help you solve problems!

 1 Read the problem carefully.

 2 What do you need to find out?

 3 What data or information is given in the problem?

 4 What data or information do you need to use?

 5 Make a plan for what to do.

 6 Follow your plan to find the answer.

 7 Check your answer. Is it correct? Put your answer into the problem to see if it works with the information given.

 8 Evaluate your method. How could you improve it next time?

What was the date yesterday?

What does the sign mean?

Bruno

Kasper

Who scored the most? Who scored the least?

Mira

Malik

Safiya

Hana

I wonder what the fastest time is for running 100 m?

Who is the shortest?

Teacher's Guide

Look at the pictures with the children and discuss the questions.
See pages 24-5 of the *Teacher's Guide* for key ideas to draw out.

11

Comparing numbers

Let's learn

83 is greater than 73 so 73 is greater than 83.

You're right, 83 **is** greater than 73, but that means that 73 is **less than** 83.

Comparing numbers

The more tens a number has, the greater it is.

If 2 numbers have the same number of tens, then look at the ones. The more ones a number has, the greater it is.

74 is greater than 58 because 74 has more tens.

58 is less than 74 because 58 has fewer tens.

tens	ones
7	4
5	8

tens	ones
7	4
7	2

74 is greater than 72.
They both have the same number of tens but 74 has more ones.

72 is less than 74 because they both have the same number of tens but 72 has fewer ones.

Ordering numbers   74 58 72 86 37 89 65 83 51

You can order numbers by comparing them to each other.

Placing numbers on a number line puts them in order from smallest to greatest.

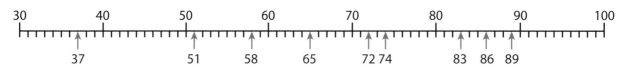

30   40   50   60   70   80   90   100

37   51   58   65   72 74   83 86 89

Teacher's Guide

Before working through the *Textbook*, study page 26 of the *Teacher's Guide* to see how the concepts should be introduced. Read and discuss the page with the children. Provide concrete resources to support exploration.

1 Compare.

Which is the greater number in each table?

tens	ones
6	1
6	4

tens	ones
5	9
5	8

tens	ones
3	5
5	5

tens	ones
7	2
8	0

Which is the smaller number in each table?

tens	ones
4	7
4	3

tens	ones
8	1
8	2

tens	ones
8	7
9	0

tens	ones
5	4
4	4

How do you know?

2 Find.

For each table, find the greater and smaller number. What do you notice?

tens	ones
9	4
9	2

tens	ones
7	8
7	9

tens	ones
5	0
6	0

tens	ones
8	7
7	7

3 Apply.

Put each group of numbers in order from the greatest to the smallest.

a   65p; 54p; 83p; 79p; 31p

b   36 cm; 41 cm; 58 cm; 48 cm; 62 cm

c   74 kg; 81 kg; 85 kg; 92 kg; 87 kg

d   78 m; 75 m; 79 m; 63 m; 71 m

e   56 l; 54 l; 57 l; 52 l; 59 l

4 Think.

Make 2 labels:

greater than 40   less than 60

Shuffle a set of 0–100 number cards. Sort the first 20 cards into 2 piles using your labels.

What do you notice? How will you deal with the problem?

Teacher's Guide

See page 27 of the *Teacher's Guide* for ideas of how to guide practice. Work through each step together as a class to develop children's conceptual understanding.

13 ⭐

Let's learn

You need:
- Base 10 apparatus
- place-value cards
- coins
- metre sticks

Partitioning a number is easy. It's just all the tens and all the ones. So 47 is 40 and 7.

It is, but you can partition numbers in other ways too. 47 is also 30 and 17, 20 and 27 or 10 and 37.

Partitioning in different ways

You usually partition numbers into tens and ones.

Look at 63.

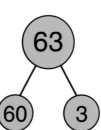

Still using tens and ones, 63 could also be

or

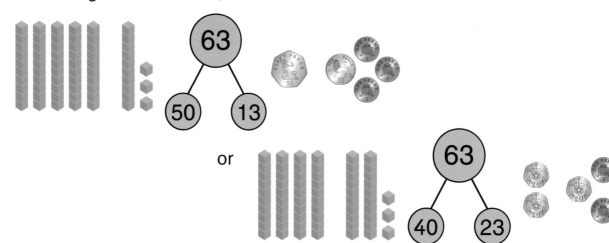

Using partitioning to solve problems

I have 37 cm of string. If I cut off 17 cm, how much string is left? **20 cm**.

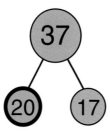

If I spend 30p, how much do I have left? **28p.**

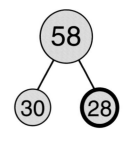

Teacher's Guide

Before working through the *Textbook*, study page 28 of the *Teacher's Guide* to see how the concepts should be introduced. Read and discuss the page with the children. Provide concrete resources to support exploration.

1 Answer.

Use these numbers to make 47, 69, 75 and 52. You can only use each number once.
Draw the partitioning trees. (19) (20) (22) (27) (30) (35) (40) (50)

2 Find.

Find 3 different ways to partition each number using tens and ones. Draw the partitioning trees. (81) (39) (94) (56)

3 Solve. Draw partitioning trees to help you solve these problems.

a   If I spend 34p, how much do I have left?

b   If I spend 40p, how much do I have left?

c   If I cut off 23 cm, how much ribbon is left?

43 cm

d   If I cut off 30 cm, how much paper is left?

79 cm

4 Think.

Complete each partitioning tree.
Write a problem to match each one.

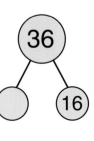

36 — 16

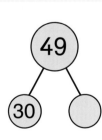

49 — 30

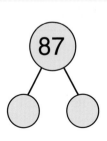

87

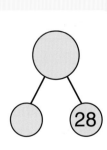

— 28

Teacher's Guide   See page 29 of the *Teacher's Guide* for ideas of how to guide practice. Work through each step together as a class to develop children's conceptual understanding.

15

Tallest, longest, shortest

Let's learn

I'm 120 cm tall, that's 1 metre and 2 centimetres.

Not quite! There are 100 centimetres in a metre, so 120 cm is 1 metre and 20 centimetres.

Measuring height and length

Your length when you are lying down is the same as your height when you are standing up.

Lucy is 125 cm tall and long.

Lucy is also 1 m 25 cm tall and long.

Comparing heights

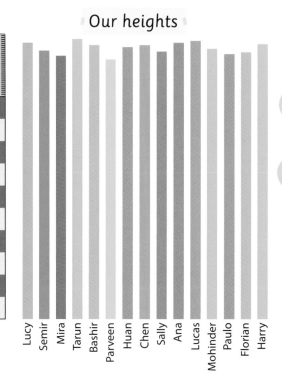

Our heights

How many children are taller than Semir?

Who is the tallest?

How many children are shorter than Sally?

Who is the shortest?

Lucy, Semir, Mira, Tarun, Bashir, Parveen, Huan, Chen, Sally, Ana, Lucas, Mohinder, Paulo, Florian, Harry

How tall (long) are you? Who is the tallest in your class?
Who is the shortest?

Teacher's Guide

Before working through the *Textbook*, study page 30 of the *Teacher's Guide* to see how the concepts should be introduced. Read and discuss the page with the children. Provide concrete resources to support exploration.

1 Answer these.

Write these heights in metres and centimetres:

a 121 cm   b 132 cm   c 109 cm   d 124 cm   e 128 cm   f 117 cm

Which is the shortest height? Which is the tallest height?

2 Answer these.

Write these lengths in centimetres only:

a 1 m 23 cm   c 1 m 11 cm   e 1 m 26 cm
b 1 m 7 cm   d 1 m 15 cm   f 1 m 5 m

Which is the shortest length? Which is the tallest length?

3 Measure.

Would you use centimetres or metres to measure the length or height of these things?

Measure the length of 1 object. Did you use the unit of measure you suggested?

4 Think.

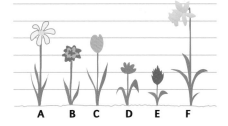

Which flower is the tallest?

Which flower is the shortest?

Write the flowers, in order from tallest to shortest.

The height of the ground is 0 cm. Each line is 10 cm higher than the one below.

Estimate how tall each plant is.

Teacher's Guide

See page 31 of the *Teacher's Guide* for ideas of how to guide practice. Work through each step together as a class to develop children's conceptual understanding.

17⭐

1d Units of time

You need:
- analogue clock
- card
- paperclips
- sharp pencils

Let's learn

I only take 2 seconds to eat my lunch so I can go out to play!

1 ... 2 ... . Have you finished yet? It's going to take at least 2 minutes!

How long does it take?

Seconds
sneeze, clap, blow your nose, write your name, yawn

Minutes
school assembly, shower, eat a sandwich, playtime, brush your teeth

Hours
school day, watching a film, sleeping at night, shopping with friends

Days
a weekend, half term

Weeks
a month, summer holidays

Class timetable

The timetable shows how much time children spend on any activity in a week.

	Monday	Tuesday	Wednesday	Thursday	Friday
	Assembly				
1 hour	English	Maths	English	Maths	Swimming
	Playtime				
1 hour	Maths	English	Maths	English	Maths
$\frac{1}{2}$ an hour	Reading	Spelling	Library	Reading	English
	Lunchtime				
1 hour	RE	Topic	PE	Topic	Topic
1 hour	PE	Topic	Topic	Topic	Topic

They do PE for an hour on Monday and an hour on Wednesday, 2 hours altogether.

Teacher's Guide

Before working through the *Textbook*, study page 32 of the *Teacher's Guide* to see how the concepts should be introduced. Read and discuss the page with the children. Provide concrete resources to support exploration.

1

Find.

How long do the activities in the first section on page 18 take?

Order the minutes activities from shortest to longest.

Order the hours activities from longest to shortest.

Activity	How long
sneeze	1 second

2

Make.

Make 2 spinners. Spin them both to make a time. Do this 3 times. Order the times from earliest to latest in the school day.

What do you do at each time?

 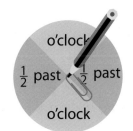

3

Solve.

Connor went to the cinema. He got home, brushed his teeth and had a shower.

Order his activities from shortest to longest.

Ruby says she spends as much time in school each day as she does sleeping each night. Is she correct?

4

Think.

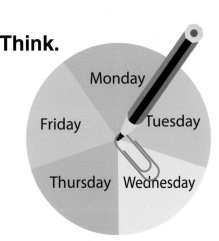

Spin all 3 spinners to get a day and a time. Look at the timetable on page 18.

What will the children be doing at that time? What do you do?

Teacher's Guide
See page 33 of the *Teacher's Guide* for ideas of how to guide practice. Work through each step together as a class to develop children's conceptual understanding.

Climb the ladder

Let's play

100

0

Teacher's Guide

See pages 34–5 of the *Teacher's Guide*. Explain the rules for each game and allow children to choose which to play. Encourage them to challenge themselves and practise what they have learnt in the unit.

100

You need:

- place-value cards 4 9
- small pieces of card or paper
- 2 large envelopes or bags
- digit cards 0–9 0 9

1 Place-value ladder

Take turns to make a 2-digit number using place-value cards and place it, in the correct order, on the ladder.

2 Digit ladder

Take turns to make a 2-digit number using digit cards and place it, in the correct order, on the ladder.

3 Your ladder

Design your own game. Explain the rules and play with a partner.

0

And finally ...

Let's review

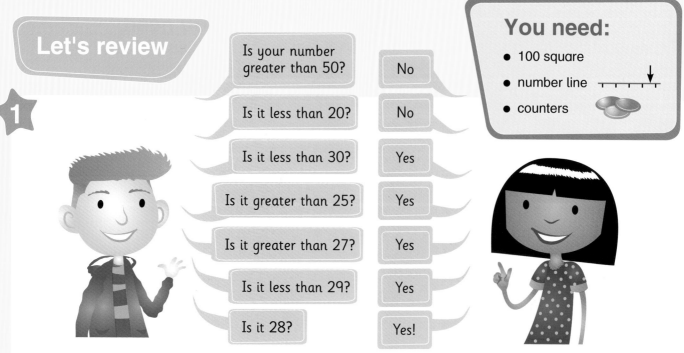

1

Is your number greater than 50?	No
Is it less than 20?	No
Is it less than 30?	Yes
Is it greater than 25?	Yes
Is it greater than 27?	Yes
Is it less than 29?	Yes
Is it 28?	Yes!

You need:
- 100 square
- number line
- counters

Play in groups of 3.

Take turns to think of a number between 0 and 100.

Your friends ask greater than or less than questions.

The player who guesses the correct number thinks of the next mystery number.

2

You need:
- Base 10 apparatus
- bead strings
- coins

If I spend 40p, how much do I have left?

Sarah used a partitioning tree to find the answer.

She says there is 26p left. Is she right?

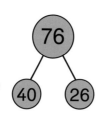

76
40   26

My piece of string is 84 cm long. If I cut off 34 cm, how much string is left?

Jack used a partitioning tree to find the answer.

He says there is 60 cm left. Is he right?

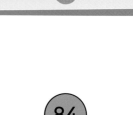

84
60   34

Teacher's Guide

See pages 36–7 of the *Teacher's Guide* for guidance on running each task. Observe children to identify those who have mastered concepts and those who require further consolidation.

3

Order these heights from shortest to tallest:

1 m 25 cm   102 cm

131 cm   123 cm

1 m 5 cm   117 cm

1 m 13 cm

Is each sentence true or false?

Our bath is 2 cm long.

My finger is 1 cm wide.

The door is about 2 m tall.

The swimming pool is 50 cm long.

My sister is 120 m tall.

Did you know?

A lot can happen in 1 minute. Your heart beats about 100 times but an elephant's heart only beats about 30 times.

In 1 minute, a snail can travel 30 cm and a hungry lizard can eat up to 45 ants, 1 at a time.

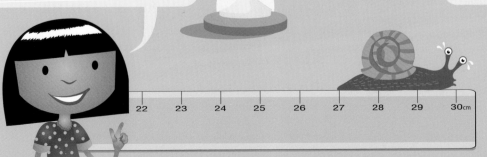

Addition and subtraction

We need 28 pencils. How many packs do we need to buy?

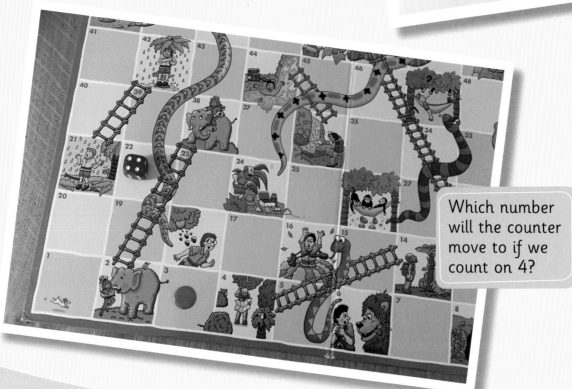

Which number will the counter move to if we count on 4?

4p 5p 6p 7p

I've got 10p! What shall I buy?

I wonder how many times you'd have to roll both dice to get a number bond for 20?

The wall is 80 cm wide. How many tiles will fit in each row?

Teacher's Guide
Look at the pictures with the children and discuss the questions.
See pages 38–9 of the *Teacher's Guide* for key ideas to draw out.

25 ★

Fact families

 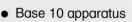
Let's learn

7 add 3 is 10 so 17 add 13 must be 20.

No! 7 add 3 is a number bond for 10. So, 17 add 3 is 20 and 7 add 13 is also 20.

Number bonds for 20

7 + 3 = 10 and the other ten makes it 17 + 3 = 20.

Can you see 3 + 17 = 20?

You can write these number bonds another way:
20 = 17 + 3 and 20 = 3 + 17.

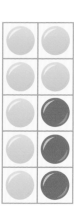

17 + 3 = 20

Fact families

Fact families are:
- the addition number statements
- the inverse subtraction number statements for that set of 3 numbers.

20	
3	17

Look again at the 2 ten frames.
Imagine all the red counters have disappeared.
Can you see 20 − 3 = 17? And 17 = 20 − 3?

Now imagine the yellow counters have disappeared.
Can you see 20 − 17 = 3? And 3 = 20 − 17?

These number facts are all in the same fact family.

17 + 3 = 20
20 = 17 + 3
7 + 13 = 20
20 = 7 + 13
20 − 3 = 17
17 = 20 − 3
20 − 17 = 3
3 = 20 − 17

Teacher's Guide

Before working through the *Textbook*, study page 40 of the *Teacher's Guide* to see how the concepts should be introduced. Read and discuss the page with the children. Provide concrete resources to support exploration.

1 Count.

Make a zero to 20 number track.
Join each number to its bond to 20, just like 9 and 11.
What do you notice?
Are there any numbers left over?

| 0 | 1 | 2 | 3 | 4 | 5 | 6 | 7 | 8 | 9 | 10 | 11 | 12 | 13 | 14 | 15 | 16 | 17 | 18 | 19 | 20 |

2 Answer this.

12 + 8 = 20. What else do you know?
What if the numbers in the bars were 20, 11 and 9?
Write the fact family.

Draw a bar model for the fact family.

| 20 | |
| 8 | 12 |

3 Measure.

Draw a target and 20 metres line on the floor. Throw a beanbag along the line to try and hit the target.

Have 3 tries. Record each try as a number fact for 20.

0   20 m

4 Think.

When you write an addition or subtraction bond for 20, you always write 5 digits.

Is Lili correct?
Explain your answer.

Teacher's Guide
See page 41 of the *Teacher's Guide* for ideas of how to guide practice.
Work through each step together as a class to develop children's conceptual understanding.

27 ⭐

Adding and subtracting ones

Let's learn

Adding ones is easy. Only the ones digit changes: 13 + 4 = 17.

Watch out! If the total number of ones is more than 10, the tens digit will change too: 13 + 8 = 21.

Adding ones

Combine ones in the augend with ones in the addend.

If there are more than 10 ones altogether, exchange 10 ones for a 10 stick to find the sum.

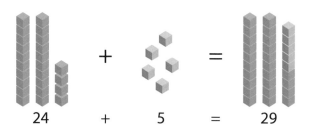

24 + 5 = 29

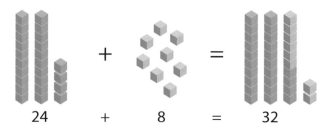

24 + 8 = 32

Adding ones is the same as counting on in ones!

Subtracting ones

If there are enough ones in the minuend, take away the correct number of ones.

If there are not enough ones in the minuend, swap a ten stick for 10 ones. Then subtract the ones.

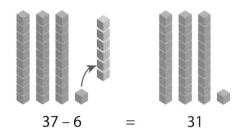

37 − 6 = 31

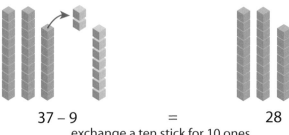

37 − 9 = 28

exchange a ten stick for 10 ones

Subtracting ones is the same as counting back in ones!

Teacher's Guide

Before working through the *Textbook*, study page 42 of the *Teacher's Guide* to see how the concepts should be introduced. Read and discuss the page with the children. Provide concrete resources to support exploration.

1 Answer these.

Complete each addition. Use Base 10 apparatus to help you. Write the matching number statement.

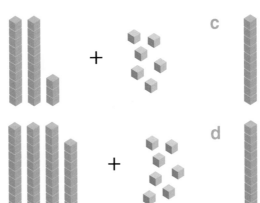
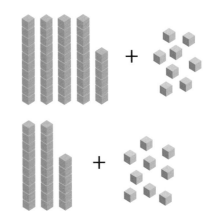

a

b

c

d

2 Answer these.

Complete each subtraction. Use Base 10 apparatus to help you. Write the matching number statement.

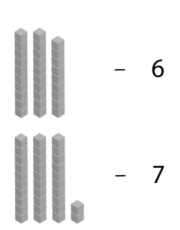
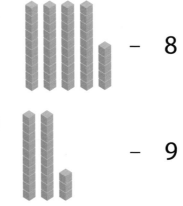

a   – 6

b   – 7

c   – 8

d   – 9

3 Apply.

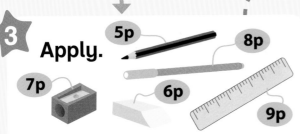

5p   8p   7p   6p   9p

Shuffle a set of digit cards.

Make a 2-digit number.

This is the amount of pence you have. Buy 1 item from the shop.

How much money do you have left?

Shuffle the cards and repeat.

4 Think. True or false?

When you subtract ones from a minuend which has more ones, the tens digit always stays the same.

When you subtract ones from a minuend which has fewer ones, the tens digit always becomes 1 less.

Explain your answers.

Teacher's Guide

See page 43 of the *Teacher's Guide* for ideas of how to guide practice. Work through each step together as a class to develop children's conceptual understanding.

You need:
- interlocking cubes
- counters
- coins 1p 5p 10p

Let's learn

Adding single-digit numbers is easy! You just look for number bonds to 10.

There won't always be a number bond to 10. You can use near bonds to 10, doubles and near doubles too.

Number bonds

Look for number bonds to 10.

If there are 2 numbers which make 10, add those first, then add on the rest.

6 + 8 + 4   6 + 4 = 10   6 + 8 + 4 = 10 + 8 = 18

Look for near bonds to 10.

 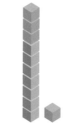

7 + 4 + 8   7 + 3 = 10, so 7 + 4 = 11   7 + 4 + 8 = 11 + 8 = 19

If there are no number bonds to 10, then make some!

⑤ + 7 + ⑧
⑤   ②   = 10 + 10 = 20

⑤ + ⑦ + 8
    ⑤   ③   = 10 + 10 = 20

Doubles or near doubles

You can also look for doubles or near doubles.

6 + 6 + 5

Double 6 is 12 and 5 more is 17.

6 + 5 is one less than double 6. 11 and 6 more is 17.

It does not matter which method you use. The total will always be the same!

Teacher's Guide

Before working through the *Textbook*, study page 44 of the *Teacher's Guide* to see how the concepts should be introduced. Read and discuss the page with the children. Provide concrete resources to support exploration.

Answer these.

Rearrange the numbers to find a number bond to 10.
Now add each set of numbers.

a   1 + 7 + 9   c   7 + 2 + 3   e   2 + 6 + 8
b   4 + 3 + 6   d   5 + 5 + 5   f   5 + 1 + 5

 Choose.

Add each set of 3 numbers. Which method will you choose?

a   5 + 2 + 3   c   1 + 5 + 8   e   4 + 2 + 7
b   9 + 3 + 3   d   7 + 4 + 7   f   5 + 6 + 7

Find a different way to add together the numbers in d and e.

 Investigate.

I have 3 coins in my pocket.
Each coin is less than 10p.
How much money could I have?

Can you find all the different possibilities?

Think.

Add 3 consecutive single-digit numbers:

1 + 2 + 3 = 6

2 + 3 + 4 = ...

3 + 4 ...

What do you notice about your totals?

Why does this happen?

Teacher's Guide

See page 45 of the *Teacher's Guide* for ideas of how to guide practice.
Work through each step together as a class to develop children's
conceptual understanding.

31

2d Adding and subtracting tens

You need:

- Base 10 apparatus
- place-value cards **4** **9**
- 100 square
- number line
- money 5p £5 1p 10p £10

Let's learn

When you add or subtract tens, only the tens digit changes.

You're partly right. The ones digit stays the same but the hundreds digit will change if you cross the hundreds barrier.

Adding tens

Partition into tens and ones and add the tens.
Put the tens together with the ones to find the total.

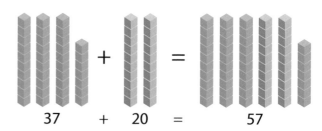

| 37 | + | 10 | = | 47 |

| 37 | + | 20 | = | 57 |

You can count on in tens to add
ten or tens! The ones digit stays the same.

Subtracting tens

Partition into tens and ones, and subtract the tens.
Put the tens together with the ones to find the difference.

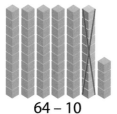 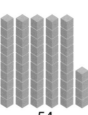 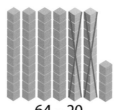 

| 64 – 10 | = | 54 |

| 64 – 20 | = | 44 |

You can count back in tens to subtract ten or tens!
The ones digit stays the same.

Teacher's Guide

Before working through the *Textbook*, study page 46 of the *Teacher's Guide* to see how the concepts should be introduced. Read and discuss the page with the children. Provide concrete resources to support exploration.

⭐**32**

1 Add. 49

Add 10, then 20, 30, 40, 50, 60 and 70 to 49.
Write the matching number statement.
Underline the first number statement which crosses the hundreds barrier.

Repeat with a different number.

2 Subtract. 134

Subtract 10, then 20, 30, 40, 50, 60 and 70 from 134.
Write the matching number statement.
Underline the first number statement which crosses the hundreds barrier.

Repeat with a different number.

3 Apply.

Each toy has £10 off in the sale.
What is the sale price of each toy?
On Super Sale Saturday, each toy has £20 off.
How much does each toy cost now?

£99
£35
£48

4 Investigate.

a 26 cm
51 cm
b
67 cm
c

1 metre = 100 cm.
Each snake grows by 10 cm in a month.
How many months will it be before each snake is more than a metre long?
How do you know?

Teacher's Guide
See page 47 of the *Teacher's Guide* for ideas of how to guide practice.
Work through each step together as a class to develop children's conceptual understanding.

33

Spin and race!

Let's play

1	2	3	4	5	6	7	8	9	10
11	12	13	14	15	16	17	18	19	20
21	22	23	24	25	26	27	28	29	30
31	32	33	34	35	36	37	38	39	40
41	42	43	44	45	46	47	48	49	50
51	52	53	54	55	56	57	58	59	60
61	62	63	64	65	66	67	68	69	70
71	72	73	74	75	76	77	78	79	80
81	82	83	84	85	86	87	88	89	90
91	92	93	94	95	96	97	98	99	100

Teacher's Guide

See pages 48–9 of the *Teacher's Guide*. Explain the rules for each game and allow children to choose which to play. Encourage them to challenge themselves and practise what they have learnt in the unit.

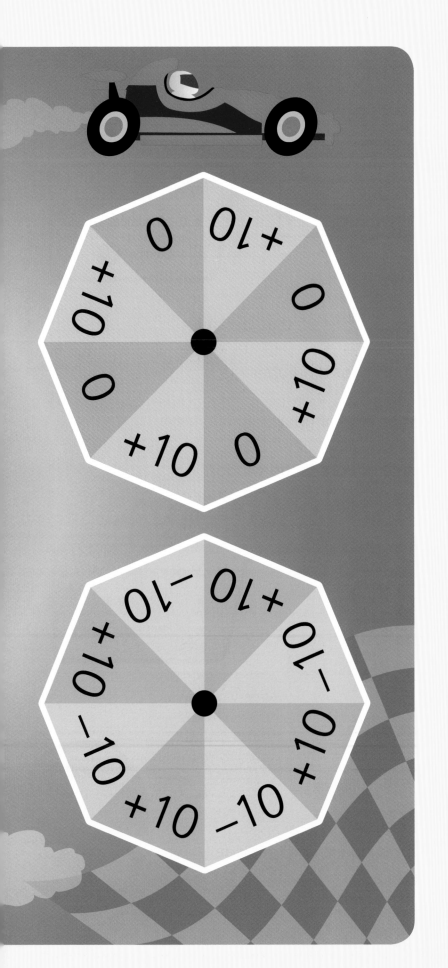

1 Add 10?

Spin to find out if you must add 10 or zero to your number. Move down your column from the Start row to Home.

2 Add or subtract 10?

Spin to find out if you must add 10 or subtract 10 from your number. Move up or down your column to reach either of the Home rows.

3 Your game

Design your own game using the gameboard. Explain the rules and play with a partner.

Let's review

1

10	

20	

You need:
- 0–20 number cards or a 1–20 dice

Draw 6 fact family bars each:
- 3 with 10 as the whole (total)
- 3 with 20 as the whole (total).

Play with a partner. Take turns to turn over a number card or to roll the dice.

Choose where to write the number on one of your sets of bars, or to miss that turn.

The first player to complete all 6 sets of bars is the winner.

2

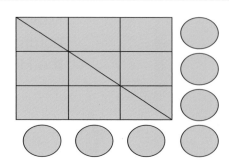

You need:
- 1–9 digit cards
- counters

Work with a partner.

Shuffle the digit cards and lay them out in a 3 by 3 grid.

Add the numbers in every row, every column and the diagonal.

Compare totals to see if you were correct.

If your partner disagrees, explain how you found your total.

Collect a counter for each correct total.

See who has collected the most counters after 3 rounds.

Teacher's Guide   See pages 50–1 of the *Teacher's Guide* for guidance on running each task.
Observe children to identify those who have mastered concepts and those who require further consolidation.

★36

3

Shuffle a set of digit cards.
Lay out 6 cards, face up, like this:

 + =

 − =

You need:
- 0–9 digit cards
- cards with + − and =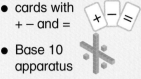
- Base 10 apparatus

Solve your number statements.

The first 2 cards make a 2-digit number.

Now set them out like this:

+ **0** =

− **0** =

Solve your number statements.

Did you know?

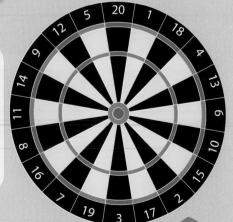

I know 3 fun facts about 20 – a group of 20 is called a score, a dartboard has 20 segments and a 3-D shape with 20 faces is called an icosahedron.

Yes, and if your dart lands in the outer ring, you win double the number of that segment. If it lands in the inner ring, you get treble (3 times) the number in that segment.
A 1–20 dice is an icosahedron.

There are lots of shapes on my desk. Which is the odd one out?

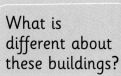

What is different about these buildings?

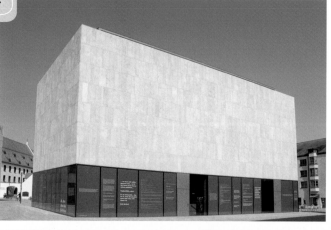

Can you see a pattern on this shell?

I wonder if both wings are the same?

Teacher's Guide
Look at the pictures with the children and discuss the questions.
See pages 52–3 of the *Teacher's Guide* for key ideas to draw out.

39 ★

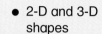
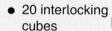

You need:

- 2-D and 3-D shapes
- 20 interlocking cubes

Let's learn

These shapes don't make a pattern because they are not in a straight line.

No, that's not right! Patterns do not always have to be in a straight line.

Making patterns

Repeating patterns can follow a rule or a mixture of rules.

This pattern is made of different shapes, colours and sizes.

The missing shape is

This pattern follows a curved path.

It also has shapes in different positions and colours.

The missing shape is

This pattern uses different 3-D shapes and colours.

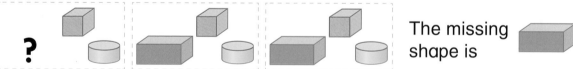

The missing shape is

Describing patterns

Describe shapes in a pattern to help find the rule.

Use the rule to find a missing shape.

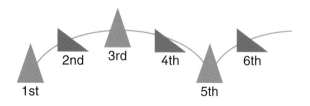

This pattern is made by using ▲ and ◣.

The 1st, 3rd and 5th shapes are purple triangles. What is the 7th shape?

The 2nd, 4th and 6th shapes are blue triangles. What is the 20th shape?

Teacher's Guide

Before working through the *Textbook*, study page 54 of the *Teacher's Guide* to see how the concepts should be introduced. Read and discuss the page with the children. Provide concrete resources to support exploration.

1 Answer these.

Look at these patterns.

a Describe the rule each pattern follows.

b Complete each pattern.

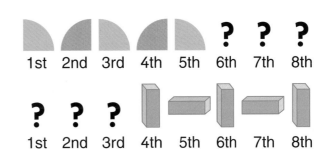

2 Identify.

Look at these patterns.

Identify the 12th shape. Explain your reasoning.

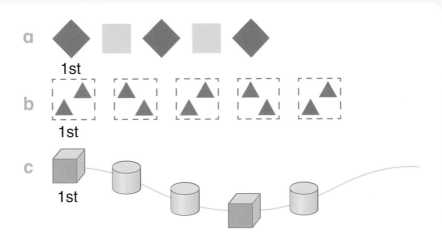

3 Apply.

Use interlocking cubes and prisms to design a row of 6 houses that follow a pattern.

How many cubes and prisms did you use?

Describe the rule that the pattern follows.

What shape would the 10th house be?

4 Think.

Make 1 easy and 1 difficult pattern using the following shapes.

Ask your partner to describe the pattern.

a

b

Teacher's Guide

See page 55 of the *Teacher's Guide* for ideas of how to guide practice. Work through each step together as a class to develop children's conceptual understanding.

41

Faces, vertices and edges

 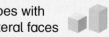
Let's learn

My square has 4 edges.

That's not right! Only 3-D shapes have edges. Your square has 4 sides.

Faces, vertices and edges of 3-D shapes

3-D shapes have vertices, faces and edges.

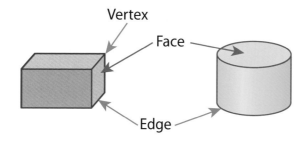

Vertex

Face

Edge

The flat faces of this cuboid are quadrilaterals.
A cylinder has curved edges and no vertex.
The flat face of the cylinder is a circle.

This is a cone.
It has a flat circular face and curved surface.

Grouping 3-D shapes

Shapes can be grouped according to their faces, vertices or edges.

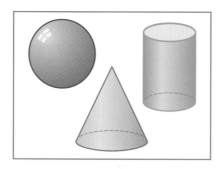

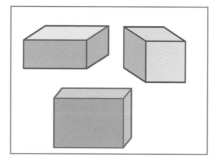

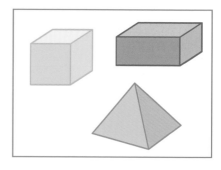

All have curved surfaces.

All have rectangular faces.

All have 5 or more vertices.

Teacher's Guide

Before working through the *Textbook*, study page 56 of the *Teacher's Guide* to see how the concepts should be introduced. Read and discuss the page with the children. Provide concrete resources to support exploration.

1 **Copy and complete.**

	Name	Number of flat faces	Number of vertices	Number of straight edges

2 **Answer this.**

Which shape is the odd one out?

a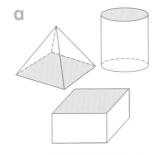

b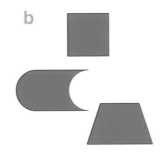

c

3 **Apply.**

Find 6 objects.

Sort them into shapes with curved surfaces and shapes with flat faces.

Now group the objects in a different way. Explain how you have grouped them.

4 **Think.**

Look at these 2 cubes. Find the number of faces, vertices and edges.

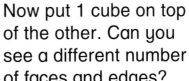

Now put 1 cube on top of the other. Can you see a different number of faces and edges?

What would happen if you place the shapes differently?

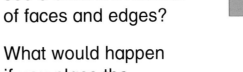

Teacher's Guide
See page 57 of the *Teacher's Guide* for ideas of how to guide practice. Work through each step together as a class to develop children's conceptual understanding.

43

Symmetry

Let's learn

I can draw a line of symmetry on both of these triangles.

No, only one of the triangles is symmetrical! You can only draw a line of symmetry when one half of the shape is a mirror image of the other.

Lines of symmetry

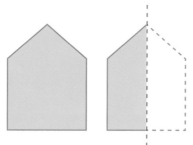

When this shape is folded, one half overlaps exactly with the other half.

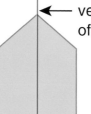

← vertical line of symmetry

This is called a vertical line because it goes straight up and down.

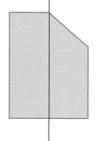

This shape does not have a line of symmetry. The halves do not match.

Symmetrical shapes

Some shapes are symmetrical.

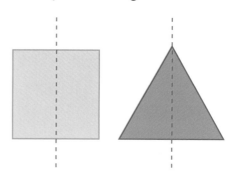

Some shapes are not symmetrical.

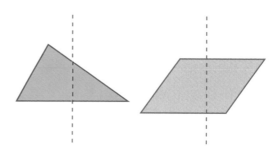

How can you check if a shape is symmetrical or not?

Teacher's Guide

Before working through the *Textbook*, study page 58 of the *Teacher's Guide* to see how the concepts should be introduced. Read and discuss the page with the children. Provide concrete resources to support exploration.

1

Identify. Which shape has a vertical line of symmetry?

a   b   c

Which shape has a vertical line of symmetry?

d   e  f

2

Copy and complete.

Copy the symmetrical shapes.
Draw 1 line of symmetry in
each shape.

a  b 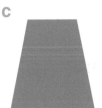 c   d

3

Make.

Fold a sheet of paper in half
vertically. Draw 2-D shapes to
make one half of a creature.
Your partner completes the
design on the other side.

How can you check your
creature is symmetrical?

Remember your
creature must be
symmetrical!

4

Investigate.

Copy the grid below. Shade 8
squares to make a shape with
only 1 vertical line of symmetry.

Now shade 8 squares to make a
shape with no lines of symmetry.

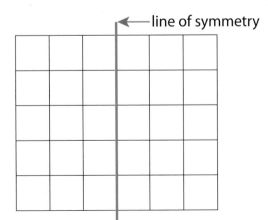
← line of symmetry

Teacher's Guide

See page 59 of the *Teacher's Guide* for ideas of how to guide practice.
Work through each step together as a class to develop children's
conceptual understanding.

45 ⭐

Game board 3

Shape hunt

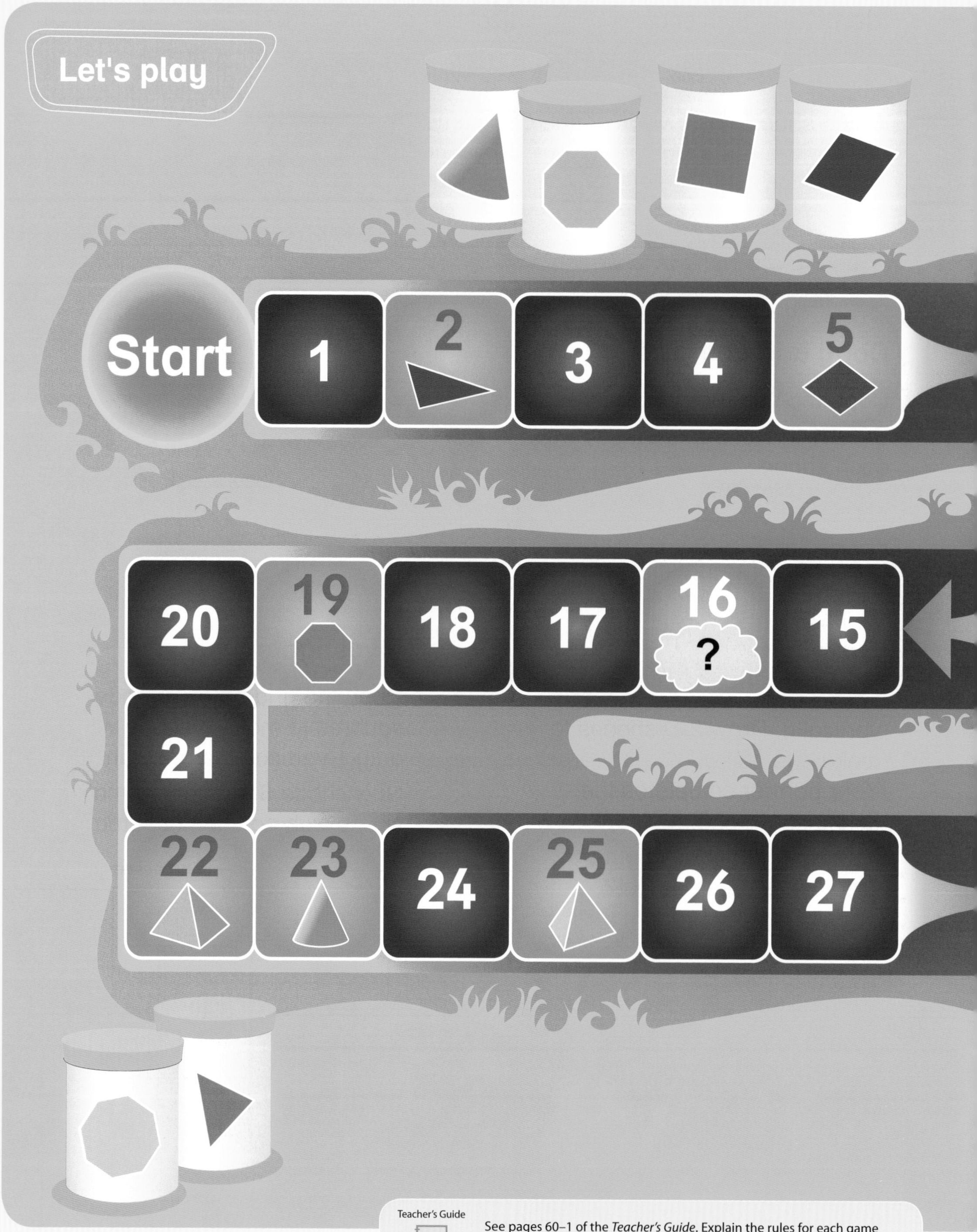
Let's play
Start
1
2
3
4
5
20
19
18
17
16
?
15
21
22
23
24
25
26
27

Teacher's Guide

See pages 60–1 of the *Teacher's Guide*. Explain the rules for each game and allow children to choose which to play. Encourage them to challenge themselves and practise what they have learnt in the unit.

You need:
- counters
- 1–6 dice

1 Shape spotter

Identify the shapes to score points.
The winner collects the most points.

2 Vertex collector

Count the vertices of the shapes you land on.
The winner collects the most points.

3 Your game

Make up your own game using the gameboard.

And finally ...

Let's review

1

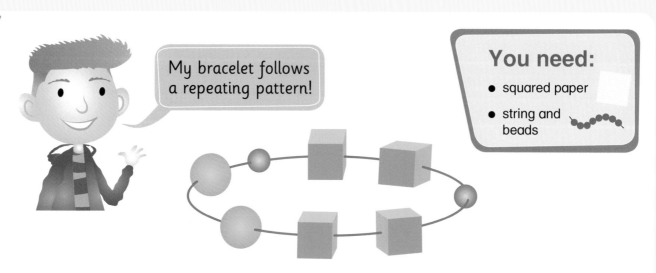

My bracelet follows a repeating pattern!

You need:
- squared paper
- string and beads

Do you agree? Explain your answer.

Rearrange the beads to make a different pattern. Describe the rule your pattern follows. If the pattern continued, what would the 10th shape be?

2

I made a cuboid using 4 long straws, 8 short straws and 8 balls of clay.

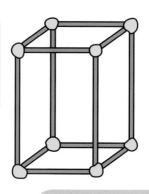

You need:
- straws
- modelling clay

What shapes can you make using: 12 straws of the same length and 8 balls of clay?

Separate the shapes into 2 groups. Explain how you grouped them. Add 2 more shapes to each group. Describe the reasons for your choice.

How many straws and balls of clay do you need to make a pyramid? Describe the faces each shape has.

Teacher's Guide

See pages 62–3 of the *Teacher's Guide* for guidance on running each task. Observe children to identify those who have mastered concepts and those who require further consolidation.

Cut a pentagon into 5 triangles.

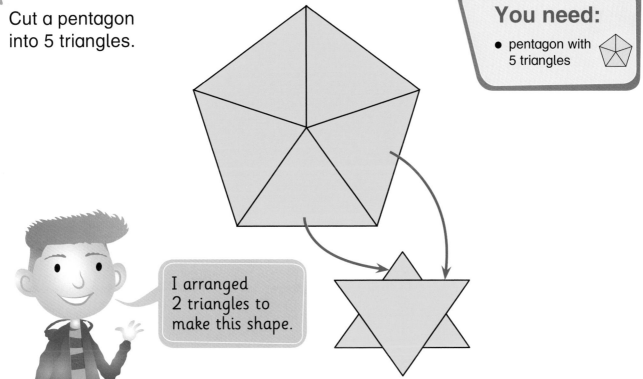

You need:
- pentagon with 5 triangles

I arranged 2 triangles to make this shape.

Rearrange the pieces to make new shapes with a vertical line of symmetry. Name the shapes you made and show clearly the vertical line of symmetry. How many different shapes can you make?

Did you know?

Diamonds are symmetrical stones. The more symmetrical the diamond is, the more sparkly and expensive it is. A small diamond called 'perfect symmetric' sold for £10 000 000 in 2011.

Symmetry is very precious indeed!

Number and measurement

Which amount is less than the others?

Is the mass of the parcel greater than or less than 5 kg?

Flapjacks recipe

200 g rolled oats
50 g caster sugar
100 g butter
100 g golden syrup

Which ingredient do you need the greatest amount of?

What time is it?

I wonder how much water is in the fish tank?

Teacher's Guide

Look at the pictures with the children and discuss the questions.
See pages 64–5 of the *Teacher's Guide* for key ideas to draw out.

51 ★

Less than and greater than

Let's learn

You can write > and < for 'is less than' and 'is greater than'. It saves a lot of writing!

Yes, but be careful to get the signs the right way round! < means 'is less than' and > means 'is greater than'.

Less than

3 ones is less than 5 ones

 3 is less than 5

3 < 5

 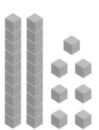

21 is less than 27

21 < 27

The numbers are ordered from smaller to greater.

Greater than

5 ones is greater than 3 ones

 5 is greater than 3

5 > 3

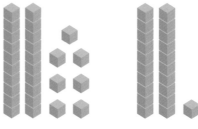

27 is greater than 21

27 > 21

The numbers are ordered from greater to smaller.

The equals sign

4 is equivalent to 4

4 = 4

 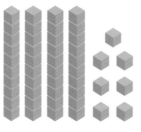 

47 = 47

Teacher's Guide

Before working through the *Textbook*, study page 66 of the *Teacher's Guide* to see how the concepts should be introduced. Read and discuss the page with the children. Provide concrete resources to support exploration.

1 Solve.

Rearrange the cards to make the statements correct.

a [<] [38] [15]   d [>] [50] [79]   g [=] [94] [94]   i [<] [53] [51]

b [>] [45] [47]   e [<] [76] [74]   h [>] [53] [51]   j [>] [82] [87]

c [<] [29] [48]   f [=] [67] [67]

> **Remember:**
> < means 'is less than'
> > means 'is greater than'
> = means 'is equal to'

2 Complete.

Copy and complete the number statements.
Use <, > or =

a 64 ___ 58   d 36 ___ 29   g 71 ___ 78

b 45 ___ 55   e 87 ___ 87   h 84 ___ 89

c 79 ___ 74   f 59 ___ 62   i 24 ___ 24

3 Apply.

Rearrange the cards to make the statements correct.
Use a ruler and metre stick to help you.

a [<] [13 cm] [19 cm]   e [>] [2 cm] [5 cm]

b [<] [17½ cm] [19 cm]   f [>] [46½ cm] [49½ cm]

c [=] [100 cm] [1 m]   g [>] [34 cm] [27 cm]

d [>] [9 cm] [15½ cm]   h [<] [52½ cm] [59½ cm]

4 Think.

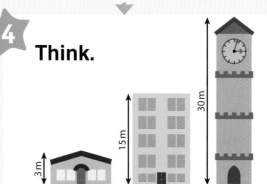

The flats are shorter than the clock tower, 15 m < 30 m

Write 4 more word and number statements about the heights of these buildings. Use < and > signs.

Teacher's Guide
See page 67 of the *Teacher's Guide* for ideas of how to guide practice.
Work through each step together as a class to develop children's conceptual understanding.

53

4b How much?

Let's learn

There are 100 centimetres in a metre, so there must be 100 grams in a kilogram.

You need:
- weights
- scales
- measuring jugs and beakers
- rice
- sand

Kilo means 1000. There are 1000 grams in a kilogram.

Mass

You measure mass in grams and kilograms.

1000 g = 1 kg

1 g   1 kg

The zoo has 6 penguins.

| 15 kg | 21kg | 7 kg | 13 kg | 11kg | 5kg |
| Charlie | George | Fred | Sarah | Cleo | Paula |

15 kg > 13 kg, so Charlie is heavier than Sarah.

7 kg < 11 kg, so Fred is lighter Cleo.

Capacity

You measure capacity in millilitres and litres.

1000 ml = 1 l

Fruit punch recipe
4 litres lemonade
1 litre mango juice
2 litres orange juice
200 ml blackcurrant juice

1 l < 2 l, so there is less mango juice than orange juice.

Teacher's Guide

Before working through the *Textbook*, study page 68 of the *Teacher's Guide* to see how the concepts should be introduced. Read and discuss the page with the children. Provide concrete resources to support exploration.

1 Answer these.

Would you use grams or kilograms to measure the mass of each item?

2 Answer these.

Would you use millilitres or litres to measure the capacity of each container?

3 Apply.

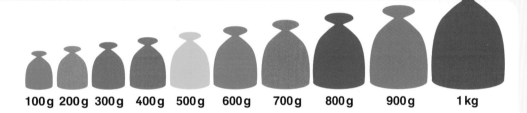

100 g 200 g 300 g 400 g 500 g 600 g 700 g 800 g 900 g 1 kg

Lili used each weight once to write 4 number statements. She added weights together to make sure she used them all.

　　 g >　　 g　　　 g <　　 g　　　 g =　　 g　　　 g =　　 g

What could her number statements have been?

Use scales and a set of weights to help you.

250 ml > 200 ml

4 Think.

Write 4 number statements about the capacities using <, > or =. Which amounts could you use to fill a 1-litre jug, without spilling any?

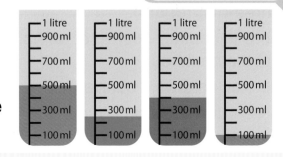

Teacher's Guide

See page 69 of the *Teacher's Guide* for ideas of how to guide practice. Work through each step together as a class to develop children's conceptual understanding.

55 ★

Quarter past and quarter to

Let's learn

I'm going to watch the clock as it gets near 11 o'clock. I want to see the hour hand jump from 10 to 11.

The hour hand moves slowly. It takes a whole hour to move from one number to the next!

Quarter past

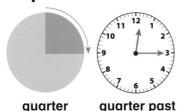

quarter   quarter past

The minute hand has made a quarter turn.

The clock shows a quarter past 12.

A quarter of an hour is 15 minutes.

Quarter to

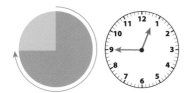

three-quarters   quarter to

The minute hand has made a three-quarter turn.

There is another quarter of an hour until the next hour.

The clock shows a quarter to 1.

Three-quarters of an hour is 45 minutes.

Half past

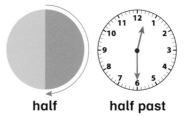

half   half past

The minute hand has made a half turn.

The clock shows half past 12.

Half an hour is 30 minutes.

There are 60 minutes in an hour.

On the hour

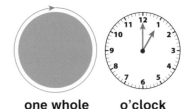

one whole   o'clock

The minute hand has made a full turn.

The clock shows 1 o'clock.

There are 24 hours in a day.

Teacher's Guide

Before working through the *Textbook*, study page 70 of the *Teacher's Guide* to see how the concepts should be introduced. Read and discuss the page with the children. Provide concrete resources to support exploration.

1 **Answer.**

Write the correct times for each picture.

Playtime starts   Playtime ends

Lunchtime starts   Lunchtime ends

Swimming starts   Swimming ends

2 **Draw.**

Draw the hands on a clock face to show these times.

a   Quarter to 6   d   Quarter past 11   g   Quarter to 12

b   Quarter to 8   e   Quarter to 4   h   Quarter past 2

c   Quarter past 9   f   Quarter to 10   i   Quarter past 7

3 **Play.**

Take it in turns to roll the dice.

Move the hands that number of quarters of an hour.

Read and write down the new time.

Continue until you reach 12 o'clock again.

4 **Think.**

Which of these clocks shows a time between 8 o'clock and 10 o'clock?

Write 2 more times between 8 o'clock and 10 o'clock.

Seb says he only needs to look at the hour hand to tell the time. How does he do this?

Teacher's Guide

See page 71 of the *Teacher's Guide* for ideas of how to guide practice. Work through each step together as a class to develop children's conceptual understanding.

57 ★

Inequalities

Let's play

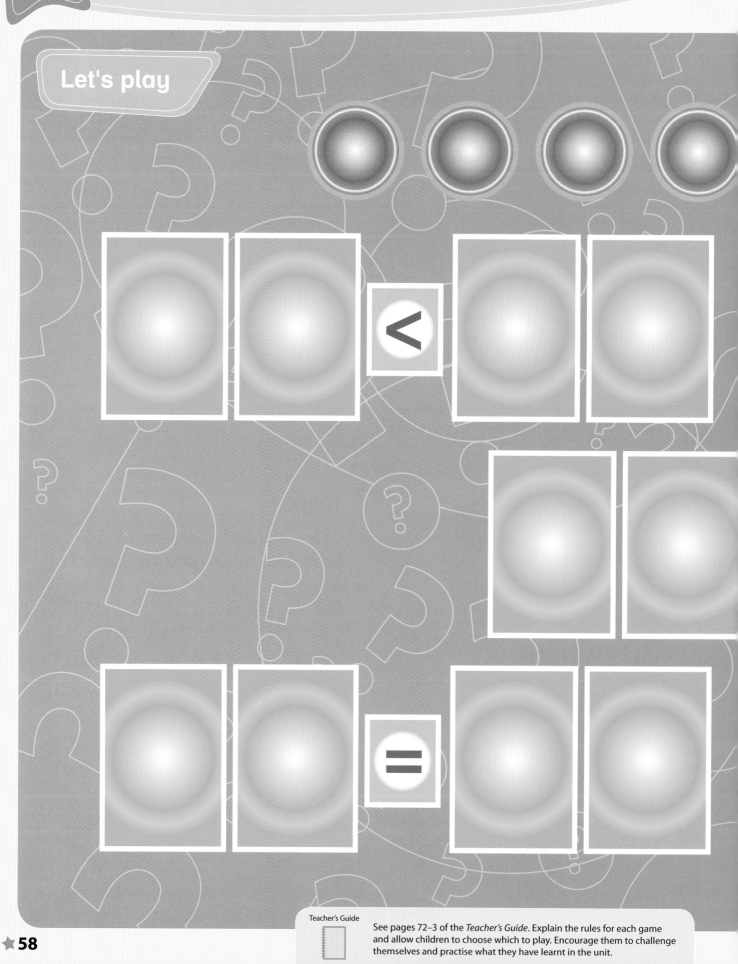

Teacher's Guide

See pages 72–3 of the *Teacher's Guide*. Explain the rules for each game and allow children to choose which to play. Encourage them to challenge themselves and practise what they have learnt in the unit.

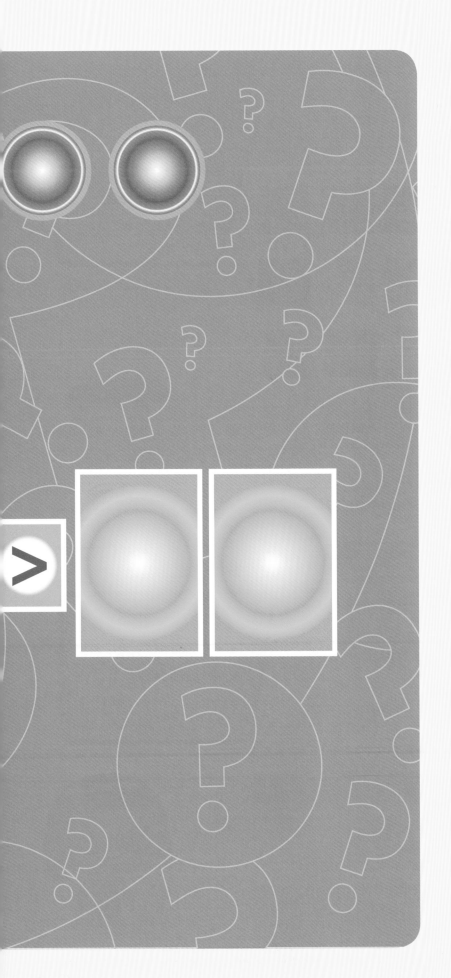

 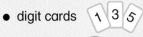
1 **Pick your place**

Choose where to put your digit cards. Can you make a correct number statement?

2 **Sort it**

What do you need to change to make the statements correct?

3 **Your game**

Make up your own game using the gameboard.

Let's review

1

6	19	21	27	27	28	39

43	48	51	51	54	57	64

72	78	78	93	<	<	<

=	=	=	>	>	>

Make 9 correct number statements.
Each number statement should use 2 numbers and a sign.

You need:
- sticky notes

Write the numbers and signs on sticky notes!

2

Sort these statements into 2 lists: true and false.

2 kg > 4 kg	50 g < 100 g
1000 kg = 1 g	5 kg > $3\frac{1}{2}$ kg
500 g = $\frac{1}{2}$ kg	1000 ml = 1 l
250 ml < 500 ml	400 ml < 200 ml
500 ml < $\frac{1}{2}$ l	

Change the false statements to make them true.

You need:
- sticky notes
- weighing scales
- litre jugs for checking

Use scales and jugs to check your answer.

Teacher's Guide

See pages 74–5 of the *Teacher's Guide* for guidance on running each task. Observe children to identify those who have mastered concepts and those who require further consolidation.

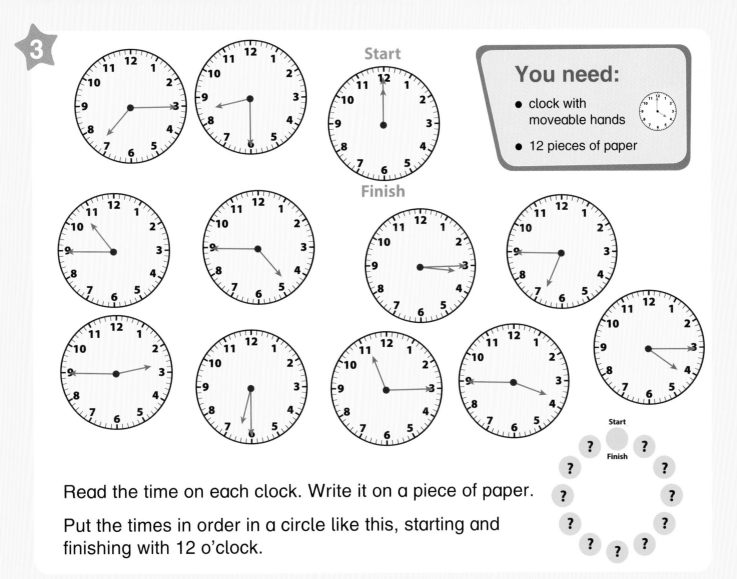

Read the time on each clock. Write it on a piece of paper.

Put the times in order in a circle like this, starting and finishing with 12 o'clock.

Did you know?

The 'is less than' and 'is greater than' signs are more than 400 years old!

They first appeared in a book written by Thomas Harriot. He was an astronomer, and may also have been responsible for bringing the potato to the UK!

Money

How much money is there?

50p

Which coins could I pay with?

I save 10p a week. I wonder how many weeks it will take to save £1?

Can you get coins and notes from a cash machine?

How much is it for 1 turn? I wonder how many turns you can have for £1?

5 turns for 50p

Teacher's Guide
Look at the pictures with the children and discuss the questions.
See pages 76–7 of the *Teacher's Guide* for key ideas to draw out.

63 ⭐

You need:
- ten frames and counters
- place-value counters
- Base 10 apparatus
- coins

Let's learn

There are 6 number bonds for 10, so there must be 60 number bonds for 100.

There are 6 number bonds for 10 but there are also 6 number bonds for 100 if you only use multiples of 10!

Number bonds for multiples of 10

If you know that $1 + 9 = 10$, you also know that:

$11 + 9 = 20$ and $1 + 19 = 20$

$21 + 9 = 30$ and $1 + 29 = 30$

$31 + 9 = 40$ and $1 + 39 = 40$

What is the same each time? What is different each time?

Once you know your number bonds for 10, you know them for any multiple of 10.

Number bonds for 100 using multiples of 10

You can use number bonds for 10 to find all the multiples of 10 to make 100.

$0 + 10 = 10 \rightarrow 0 + 100 = 100$

$1 + 9 = 10 \rightarrow 10 + 90 = 100$

$2 + 8 = 10 \rightarrow 20 + 80 = 100$

$3 + 7 = 10 \rightarrow 30 + 70 = 100$

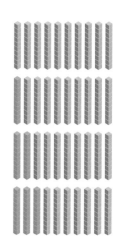

Teacher's Guide

Before working through the *Textbook*, study page 78 of the *Teacher's Guide* to see how the concepts should be introduced. Read and discuss the page with the children. Provide concrete resources to support exploration.

1

Add.

Use Base 10 apparatus to help you.

Choose 1 of these number bonds as your starting point.
Continue the pattern to 100.

$2 + 8 = 10$ $7 + 3 = 10$ $4 + 6 = 10$

2

Answer these.

Copy the number line.
Draw an arrow to join each multiple of 10 to its number bond for 100.
Are there any numbers left over?

0   10   20   30   40   50   60   70   80   90   100

Write the 4 addition number statements for each number bond.
Which number bond is missing? Why?

3

Apply.

Choose a number bond
from Step 1.

Turn it into a number bond
for 100 using multiples of 10.

Find 3 different ways to show
your number bond using
only 10p, 20p and 50p coins.

4

Think.

Use exactly 4 coins to show
each number bond for 100
using multiples of 10.

You can only
use 10p, 20p
and 50p coins.

Teacher's Guide   See page 79 of the *Teacher's Guide* for ideas of how to guide practice.
Work through each step together as a class to develop children's
conceptual understanding.

65

5b Pounds and pence

You need:
- money
- metre stick
- ruler
- 100 square

Let's learn

My gran gave me a £5 note. I've got more money than you because you've only got coins.

No, I've got three £2 coins, that's £6. So I've got more money than you!

Coins and bank notes

These are all the coins and bank notes used in the United Kingdom.

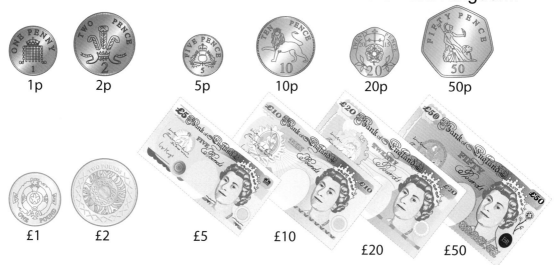

1p   2p   5p   10p   20p   50p

£1   £2   £5   £10   £20   £50

The unit symbol for pence is p. The unit symbol for pound is £.

Remember, there are 100 pence in £1.

Look at the different values. What do you notice?

Same value

You can make the same value in lots of different ways

What do you notice?

Teacher's Guide

Before working through the *Textbook*, study page 80 of the *Teacher's Guide* to see how the concepts should be introduced. Read and discuss the page with the children. Provide concrete resources to support exploration.

1 Make the amount.

Make each amount in 2 different ways. Use coins and bank notes.

a   60p   b   £60   c   36p   d   £36   e   53p   f   £53

2 Calculate.

Lili bought a pencil for 35p.
She paid with silver coins.
Find the 5 ways she could have paid for the pencil.

3 Solve.

You have 1 of each of these coins.

At the shop, everything costs less than £1.

You have to pay using the exact amount of money.

Which amounts could you pay?

Use a 100 square to record your results.

✔	✔	✔	✘	✔	✔		
1	2	3	4	5	6	7	8

4 Investigate.

Would you rather have a metre of 2p coins or 30 cm of 10p coins?

Find out which length of coins has the greater value.

Use a metre stick, a ruler, 2p and 10p coins to help you.

Remember
£1 = 100p

Teacher's Guide

See page 81 of the *Teacher's Guide* for ideas of how to guide practice.
Work through each step together as a class to develop children's conceptual understanding.

67 ★

Adding and subtracting money

You need:
- money
- Base 10 apparatus
- bead string
- number line
- 3-D shapes
- 1-6 dice

Let's learn

Adding money is more difficult than adding numbers.

It's just as easy! Just use your number bonds.

Adding with money

Numbers work in the same way whatever you are adding.

26 + 7 =	26p + 7p =	£26 + £7 =
26 + 4 + 3 =	26p + 4p + 3p =	£26 + £4 + £3 =
30 + 3 = 33	30p + 3p = 33p	£30 + £3 = £33

Can you think of some different ways to add?

Subtracting with money

Numbers work in the same way whatever you are subtracting.

33p – 7p =
33p – 3p – 4p =
30p – 4p = 26p

What has changed?

£33 – £7 = £26

What has changed?

Teacher's Guide

Before working through the *Textbook*, study page 82 of the *Teacher's Guide* to see how the concepts should be introduced. Read and discuss the page with the children. Provide concrete resources to support exploration.

1 Calculate.

Use a different method or representation each time.

Find the total of each amount of money.

a   £45 + £3
b   £45 + £30
c   £45 − £3
d   £45 − £30
e   37p + 6p
f   37p + 60p
g   37p − 6p
h   37p − 30p

2 Calculate.

Seb had 50p to spend in the school shop this week. He bought 1 fruit each day. On Friday he had 2p left. What could he have bought each day?

orange 23p

banana 12p

pear 10p

apple 16p   plum 8p

3 Solve.

Add the price of every face to find the cost of each 3-D shape.

2-D shape prices
Square or rectangle 10p
Triangle 12p
Circle 18p

Special offer:
For all curved surfaces subtract 10p from your total cost (not including spheres!)

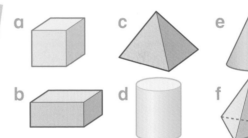

a   c   e

b   d   f

4 Think.

Use a 1p, 2p, 5p 10p or 20p coin as your starting amount.

| coin | Roll a dice to find out how many tens to add to your amount. | Record your total so far. | Roll the dice again to find out how many ones to subtract from your total so far. | Record your total so far. |

Find 4 totals. Use a different starting coin each time.

What was your highest amount? What was your lowest amount?

Teacher's Guide

See page 83 of the *Teacher's Guide* for ideas of how to guide practice.
Work through each step together as a class to develop children's
conceptual understanding.

69 ⭐

Money problems

Let's learn

You need:
- money 5p 1p 10p £5 £10

My Dad always pays the exact amount with his bank card. You must have to pay the exact amount with money too.

That's not true! When you pay with money you can pay too much and get some money back.

Change

When you buy something and pay with a larger-value coin or note, you get some money back called change.

Seb bought a pencil for 12p. He gave the shopkeeper a 20p coin.
Find the difference to work out the change.
Count up from 12p, count back from 20p, use
a number bond or calculate in a different way.
20p − 12p = 8p

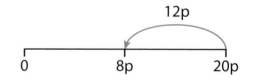

Which coins could you use to give Seb his change?

Solving money problems

If you are not sure if you need to add or subtract, use the bar model.

Seb bought a CD for £8 and a book for £6.
How much did he spend?
Add £8 and £6 to find out.
£8 + £6 = £14

Lili spent £14 on a CD and a book.
How much change did she get from £20?
Subtract £14 to find out.

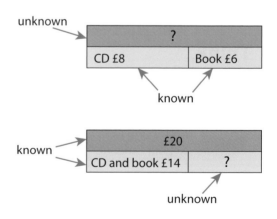

Teacher's Guide

Before working through the *Textbook*, study page 84 of the *Teacher's Guide* to see how the concepts should be introduced. Read and discuss the page with the children. Provide concrete resources to support exploration.

1 Calculate.

Each customer pays for their lunch with a £20 note.
How much change do they get?

a   Sandwich £2

b   Burrito £7

Each customer pays for their drink with a 50p coin.
How much change do they get?

c   Coffee 48p

d   Tea 34p

2 Calculate.

Each customer pays for their shopping with a £20 note.
How much change do they get?

a   CD £7 and sweets £1

b   Cinema ticket £6, popcorn £3, drink £3

Each customer pays for their shopping with a £50 note.
How much change do they get?

c   Jumper £19, jeans £29

d   Jacket £35, scarf £6

3 Apply.

Parking £4 per hour

The parking metre only takes £5, £10 and £20 notes.
It does not give change.
How long can you park using each bank note?

What is the cheapest way to pay to park for 2, 3, 4 and 5 hours? How much extra time will you pay for each time?

4 Investigate.

You have £1 (100p) to spend at the school stationery shop.

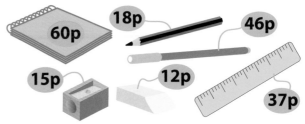

How much change would you get if you bought 3 items?

Teacher's Guide

See page 85 of the *Teacher's Guide* for ideas of how to guide practice. Work through each step together as a class to develop children's conceptual understanding.

Race to riches!

Let's play

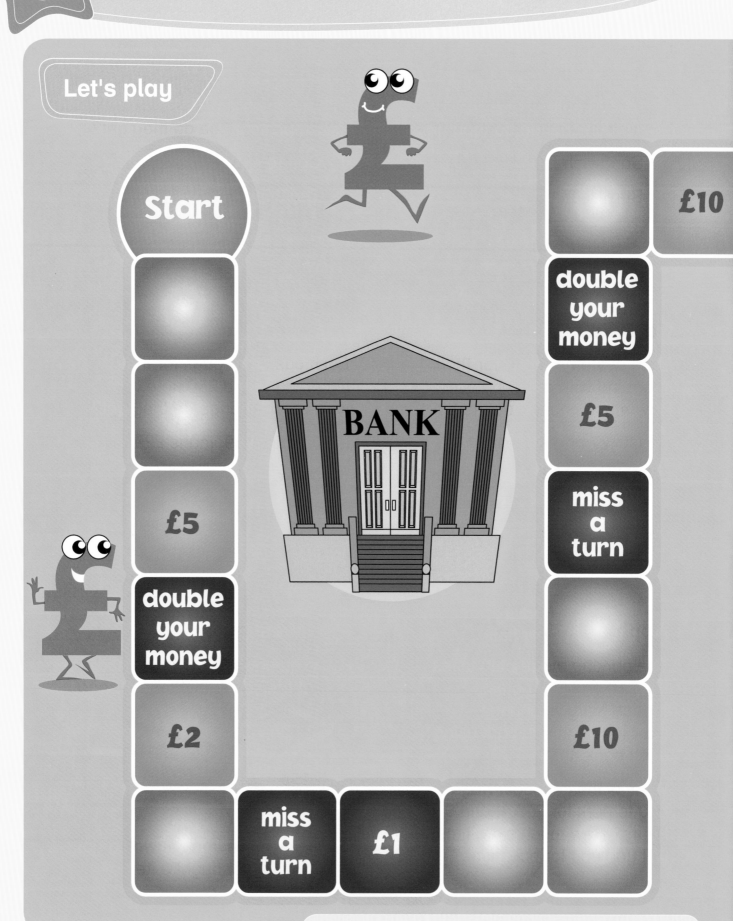

Start

£5

double
your
money

£2

miss
a
turn

£1

BANK

double
your
money

£5

miss
a
turn

£10

£10

Teacher's Guide

See pages 86–7 of the *Teacher's Guide*. Explain the rules for each game
and allow children to choose which to play. Encourage them to challenge
themselves and practise what they have learnt in the unit.

1 Money trail

Race around the board collecting money. Who will have the most by the Finish?

2 Find some, lose some

Land on a money square. Spin to find out whether you keep the money or give it away!

3 Your game

Design your own game using the gameboard. Explain the rules and play with a partner.

And finally ...

Let's review

1

28 + 2 = 30 is the last number statement in a pattern of calculations which began with a number bond for 10:

$$8 + 2 = 10 \rightarrow 18 + 2 = 20 \rightarrow 28 + 2 = 30$$

Write the pattern of calculations for each number statement.

a 8 + 32 = 40

b 24 + 6 = 30

c 65 + 5 = 70

d 0 + 100 = 100

e 9 + 41 = 50

Which number bond for 10 is left over?

Use this number bond as the first number statement in a pattern 6 statements long.

2

Place all the coins in a bag or envelope.

Tip out 2 coins. Add them together.

Subtract the smaller value coin from the larger value coin.

Return the coins to the bag and repeat.

Draw a set of bars for 1 of your additions.

You need:

• 1p, 2p, 5p, 10p, 20p, 50p coins

• feely bag or envelope

What are the smallest and largest totals you can make?
What are the smallest and largest differences you can make?

Now tip out 3 coins.
Find the total of the 3 coins.
Add 2 coins together and subtract the third. *Or* Subtract 2 coins from the highest value coin.
What are the smallest and largest totals you can make?
What are the smallest and largest differences you can make?

Teacher's Guide

See pages 88–9 of the *Teacher's Guide* for guidance on running each task.
Observe children to identify those who have mastered concepts and those who require further consolidation.

3

Stamps cost £1, £2, £5, £10, £20, and £50 at the Pound Post Office.

You have 3 parcels to post.
They cost £8, £7 and £4 to post.
Which stamps should you buy?

If you pay with a £20 note, how much change will you get?

You need:
- stamps
- large envelopes

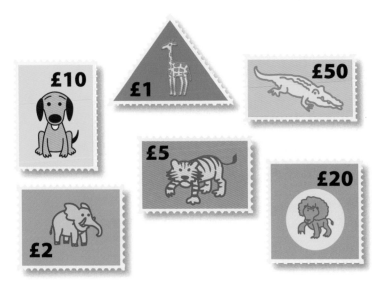

Oh no! They've sold out of £5 stamps. Which stamps should you buy now?

Did you know?

New coins and bank notes are sometimes produced, for special occasions. A £20 coin and a £100 coin were made in 2015 to celebrate Queen Elizabeth II becoming the longest reigning monarch in the UK. They were for keeping not spending.

Some £5 coins were made too, but the gold one cost £1650! That's a lot more than £5!

75

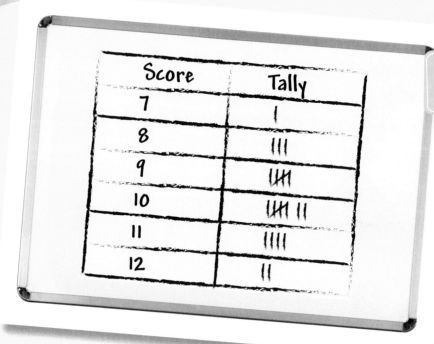

Score	Tally
7	I
8	III
9	IIII
10	IIIII II
11	IIII
12	II

What are those marks?

I wonder how many are left?

Is that an odd or even number?

I wonder which pile is worth the most?

I wonder how many more cups you could fill from the jug?

Teacher's Guide

Look at the pictures with the children and discuss the questions.
See pages 90–1 of the *Teacher's Guide* for key ideas to draw out.

77

Estimating

Let's learn

Wow, this snake must be at least 10 metres long!

I think it's nearer 2 metres long. Think about how long the metre stick is.

Estimating how many

An estimate is a sensible guess.

To make an estimate, use what you already know.

Sometimes you know how many items a full container holds.

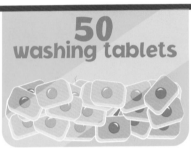

This box looks half full.

About 25?

Sometimes you can look at 1 object and think how many there could be of the same size.

About 35? 40?

Estimating measures

Make sure you know what some everyday measures look and feel like.

This will help you make estimates.

1 metre stick

30 cm ruler

Chocoh! 100g

Hand Gel 100 ml

RICE 1kg

lemonade 1 litre

Teacher's Guide

Before working through the *Textbook*, study page 92 of the *Teacher's Guide* to see how the concepts should be introduced. Read and discuss the page with the children. Provide concrete resources to support exploration.

★ 78

1 **Estimate.**

Estimate how many sweets are left in each jar.

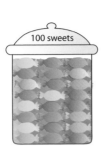
100 sweets

Check with a friend.
Are your estimates similar?

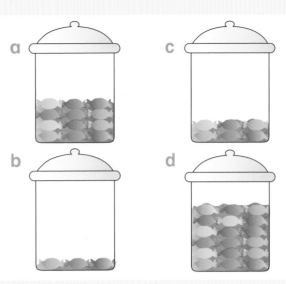
a

c

b

d

2 **Estimate.**

Estimate the length of each pencil.

a   b

c

d

Measure the length of each pencil.
Compare the measurements with your estimates.

3 **Measure.**

Estimate $\frac{1}{2}$ a litre of water in each bottle.

Pour the water into a jug to check.

Estimate $\frac{1}{4}$ litre (250 ml) and $\frac{3}{4}$ litre (750 ml).

Is it easier to estimate with the 1-litre or 2-litre bottle?

You need:
- water
- empty 1-litre and 2-litre bottles
- measuring jug

4 **Think.**

Draw a straight line like this one. Use a ruler.

0   100

Use what you know about $\frac{1}{4}$, $\frac{1}{2}$ and $\frac{3}{4}$ to mark 25, 50 and 75 on your number line.

Estimate and mark 10, 40, 60, 90 and 3 more numbers.

Teacher's Guide

See page 93 of the *Teacher's Guide* for ideas of how to guide practice. Work through each step together as a class to develop children's conceptual understanding.

79 ⭐

6b Odd and even

Let's learn

You need:
- dominoes
- coins and notes

Half must be an even number because the 2 in the denominator is even.

Fractions can't be odd or even. Only whole numbers can be odd or even.

Odd and even numbers

All even numbers are multiples of 2. They can be divided into groups of 2 with nothing left over.

Any number with a ones digit of 2, 4, 6, 8 or 0 is even.

twos

Odd numbers are not multiples of 2. When you divide them into twos, there is 1 left over.

Any number with a ones digit of 1, 3, 5, 7 or 9 is odd.

Carroll diagrams

Use a Carroll diagram to sort numbers.
All numbers are either odd or not odd (even).
All numbers are either less than 50 or not less than 50.

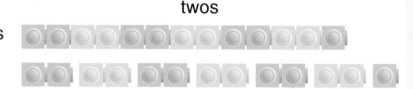

	odd	not odd
< 50	23	18
not < 50	57	92

Teacher's Guide

Before working through the *Textbook*, study page 94 of the *Teacher's Guide* to see how the concepts should be introduced. Read and discuss the page with the children. Provide concrete resources to support exploration.

⭐ **80**

Answer these.

Write the next even number after each door number.

Write the largest even number you can think of.
Now write another. And another!

Answer these.

Write the next odd number after each door number.

Write the largest odd number you can think of.
Now write another. And another!

Solve.

Copy the Carroll diagram and sort 1 of each coin and bank note onto it.

	even	not even
< 50p		
not < 50p		

What do you notice?

Investigate.

a Find these types of domino.
   Add the number of spots together on each domino. What do you notice?

b Now find these types of domino.
   Add the number of spots together on each domino. What do you notice?

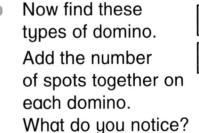

Teacher's Guide

See page 95 of the *Teacher's Guide* for ideas of how to guide practice.
Work through each step together as a class to develop children's
conceptual understanding.

81

Let's learn

Tally marks are collected in groups of 4. I can count them easily: 4, 8, 12, 16, 17, 18.

⠀卌 卌 卌 卌 ||

No, they're in groups of 5. The fifth tally is that line across the four marks. So it's 5, 10, 15, 20, 21, 22.

Block diagrams

Block diagrams use blocks to display information.

Ben rolled a dice and wrote the number down each time.

5, 4, 2, 6, 2, 1, 3, 5, 2, 1

He used his list to draw a block diagram.

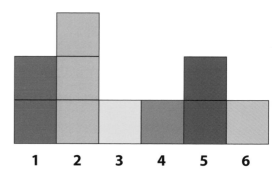

It shows Ben rolled 2 the most and 3, 4 and 6 the least.

Pictograms

A pictogram uses pictures to represent information.

Walk	☺☺☺☺☺☺☺☺☺☺☺☺
Car	☺☺☺☺☺☺☺☺☺
Bicycle	☺☺
Bus	☺☺☺
Taxi	☺☺

Key: ☺ = 1 child

If the key changed so that ☺ = 2 children, that would mean 24 children walk to school.

The tally chart and frequency table shows the same information as the pictogram.

Travel	Tally	Frequency
Walk	卌 卌 ||	12
Car	卌 ||||	9
Bicycle	||	2
Bus	|||	3
Taxi	||	2

Teacher's Guide

Before working through the *Textbook*, study page 96 of the *Teacher's Guide* to see how the concepts should be introduced. Read and discuss the page with the children. Provide concrete resources to support exploration.

1

Answer these. Each child put a cube on their birthday month.

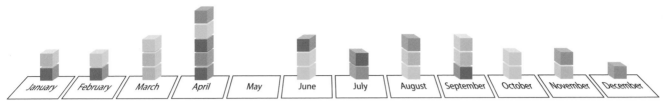

a   How many children are in the class?

b   Which month were most children born in?

c   Copy and complete a frequency table for each month.

Month	Frequency
January	2
February	

2

Answer these.

Each child drew their favourite fruit.
They made a pictogram.

a   Draw the tally chart and frequency table for this pictogram.

b   How many children are in the class?

c   What if each picture represented 2 children?
Draw a new tally chart and frequency chart.

Apple

Orange

Banana

Strawberry

Pear

3

Draw.

Take a large handful of coins.

Coin	Tally
1p	
2p	

Draw a tally chart for your coins.
Draw a block diagram to show how many you have of each coin.

4

Investigate.

Collect information from your classmates. Decide which diagram to use to display it.

Teacher's Guide

See page 97 of the *Teacher's Guide* for ideas of how to guide practice.
Work through each step together as a class to develop children's conceptual understanding.

83 ★

Escape!

Let's play

1	2	3	4	5	6
20	19	18	17	16	15
21	22	23	24	25	26
40	39	38	37	36	35
41	42	43	44	**Start**	
60	59	58	57		
61	62	63	64	65	66
80	79	78	77	76	75
81	82	83	84	85	86
100	99	98	97	96	95

236

Teacher's Guide   See pages 98–9 of the *Teacher's Guide*. Explain the rules for each game and allow children to choose which to play. Encourage them to challenge themselves and practise what they have learnt in the unit.

7	8	9	10
14	13	12	11
27	28	29	30
34	33	32	31
47	48	49	50
54	53	52	51
67	68	69	70
74	73	72	71
87	88	89	90
94	93	92	91

1 Way out

Travel along an odd or even path to escape the 100 square.

2 Path maker

Use your counters to build a path across the 100 square to the centre.

3 Your game

Make up your own game using the gameboard.

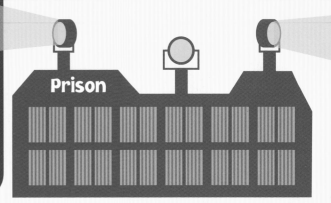

Prison

And finally ...

1

a Using 2 hands, scoop up as many counters as you can.

Estimate how many.

Now count the counters. How close was your estimate? Repeat.

b Choose 3 objects.

Estimate the length of each object.

Measure the lengths. Compare with your estimates.

How close was your estimate?

You need:
- counters
- coloured pencils, scissors, glue sticks or other classroom objects
- ruler

2

You need:
- 0–20 number cards

2 odd numbers have a total of 20.

What could the 2 odd numbers be? Find all the possible solutions.

What if the total was 30?

Find all the possible solutions.

Use the results for 20 to help you find solutions for 30.

Teacher's Guide

See pages 100–1 of the *Teacher's Guide* for guidance on running each task. Observe children to identify those who have mastered concepts and those who require further consolidation.

a Write 4 sentences about the pictogram.
Use some of these words.

more than

fewer than

most

least

same

as many as

Use words of your own as well.

b How would your sentences
change if ⚽ = 2 goals?
Draw a block diagram where
1 block = 2 goals.
How is the block diagram the
same as the pictogram?
How are they different?

Goals scored in the Year 2 football tournament

Oliver	⚽⚽⚽⚽⚽
Max	⚽⚽⚽
Jack	⚽⚽⚽⚽
Joshua	⚽
Poppy	⚽⚽⚽⚽
Ella	⚽⚽⚽
Daisy	⚽⚽
Emma	⚽⚽⚽⚽

Key: ⚽ = 1 goal

Did you know?

We can use pictures to give information quickly.

From the icons on a phone, to road signs and toilet doors, they are everywhere!

Multiplying and dividing

How many
fingers?

How many
cakes in
each tin?

What is in each hoop?

I wonder what the buttons do?

Is it 12 o'clock?

Teacher's Guide

Look at the pictures with the children and discuss the questions.
See pages 102–3 of the *Teacher's Guide* for key ideas to draw out.

89 ⭐

Repeated addition and subtraction

You need:
- counters
- arrays ⁙
- bead string
- coins
- weights
- balance scales

Let's learn

5 + 5 + 5 + 5 + 5 + 5 = 30.
I counted in fives.

You are right, but it's quicker to use multiplication facts: 5 × 6 = 30.

Repeated addition

There are 5 cups on each tray. There are 3 trays.

5 + 5 + 5 = 15

5 three times equals 15 altogether.

There's a much shorter way to write that: 5 × 3 = 15.

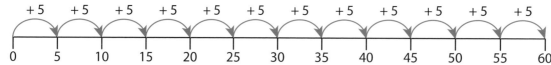

Now there are 10 trays each with 5 cups.

What is the shorter way to write this?

Repeated subtraction

60 drinks are ready for a party. 5 drinks are placed on each tray. Each time a tray is filled, 5 drinks are subtracted from the total number of drinks.

60 − 5 − 5 − 5 − 5 − 5 − 5 − 5 − 5 − 5 − 5 − 5 − 5 = 0

There's a much shorter way to write that: 60 ÷ 5 = 12

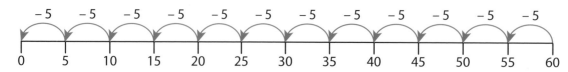

60 divided into groups of 5 equals 12 groups.

Teacher's Guide

Before working through the *Textbook*, study page 104 of the *Teacher's Guide* to see how the concepts should be introduced. Read and discuss the page with the children. Provide concrete resources to support exploration.

★ **90**

1

Answer these.

Solve these repeated addition number statements.

a 2 + 2 + 2 = ▢

c 10 + 10 + 10 + 10 + 10 = ▢

b 5 + 5 + 5 + 5 = ▢

d 5 + 5 + 5 + 5 + 1 + 4 = ▢

Now write them as multiplication statements.

2

Answer these.

Write a repeated subtraction statement and a division statement for each number line.

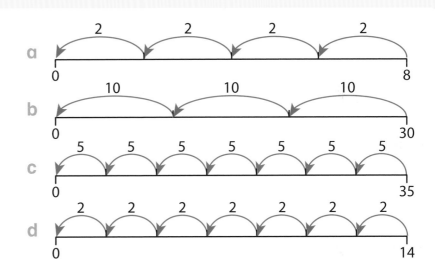

3

Record.

Write a repeated addition or a multiplication number statement for each bag of coins.

4

Investigate.

Lili has some 2 g, 5 g and 10 g weights. She weighed out 20 g of flour using just 1 type of weight. How did she do it? Find 3 different ways. Record using multiplication statements.

Choose a mass which is a multiple of 10 g and explore it in the same way.

Teacher's Guide

See page 105 of the *Teacher's Guide* for ideas of how to guide practice. Work through each step together as a class to develop children's conceptual understanding.

91 ★

Let's learn

I know 2 × 5 = 10 and 5 × 2 = 10. That means 10 ÷ 2 = 5, so 2 ÷ 10 = 5 must be right too.

You need:
- counters
- number line
- coins   5p   1p   10p
- bead string

No, division cannot be done in any order. Think about sharing 10 biscuits between 2 people, or sharing 2 biscuits between 10 people!

Multiplication tables

You can use pairs of shoes to help you count in twos and create the multiplication table for 2.

2 = 2	2 × 1 = 2
2 + 2 = 4	2 × 2 = 4
2 + 2 + 2 = 6	2 × 3 = 6
2 + 2 + 2 + 2 = 8	2 × 4 = 8

If you carry on to 12 pairs of shoes, you will have written the multiplication table for 2!

Remember, multiplicand × multiplier = product

Arrays

Here is an array made from 2 rows of 5.

5
+
5
= 10

5 + 5 = 10
5 × 2 = 10

So, 5 × 2 = 10 and 2 × 5 = 10.
Can you see 10 ÷ 2 = 5 and 10 ÷ 5 = 2?

This time the array is made from 5 rows of 2.

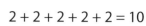

2
+
2
+
2
+
2
+
2
= 10

2 + 2 + 2 + 2 + 2 = 10
2 × 5 = 10

It's a multiplication and division fact family!

Teacher's Guide

Before working through the *Textbook*, study page 106 of the *Teacher's Guide* to see how the concepts should be introduced. Read and discuss the page with the children. Provide concrete resources to support exploration.

1   Answer these.

Copy and complete the multiplication table facts. Write out the multiplication tables for 2, 5 and 10 to help you.

a   2 × 5 =

b   3 × 10 =

c   × 8 = 16

d   × 5 = 30

e   7 × 2 =

f   × 5 = 50

g   11 × = 22

h   × 10 = 70

i   × 12 = 60

2   Answer.

Write 2 addition, 2 multiplication and 2 division number statements to match this array.

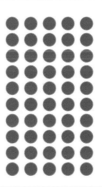

3   Solve.

a   A pear costs 10p. How much do 8 pears cost?

b   Plums cost 5p each. How much do 12 plums cost?

c   Strawberries cost 2p. How much do 11 strawberries cost?

d   An apple costs 12p. How much do 2 apples cost?

Record your solutions in multiplication statements.

4   Investigate.

Look at the products for the multiplication tables for 2, 5 and 10.

2 × 1 =	5 × 1 =	10 × 1 =
2 × 2 =	5 × 2 =	10 × 2 =
2 × 3 =	5 × 3 =	10 × 3 =
2 × 4=	5 × 4 =	10 × 4 =

What do you notice about the pattern of odd and even numbers?

Where can you see doubles?

What else do you notice?

Teacher's Guide

See page 107 of the *Teacher's Guide* for ideas of how to guide practice. Work through each step together as a class to develop children's conceptual understanding.

93

You need:

- counters
- cubes
- paper plates
- number line
- bead string
- weights
- balance scales

Let's learn

We shared a packet of 12 sweets. I had 4 and my sister had 8. So is 12 shared between 2 people 4 or 8?

In division as sharing, everyone gets the same. You should both have had 6 sweets, because 12 ÷ 2 = 6.

Division as sharing

A bag of 20 marbles is shared equally between 5 children.   20 ÷ 5 =

When sharing, you know how many you are sharing between but not how many each, so you move 1 object at a time.

They each get 4 marbles.

20 ÷ 5 = 4

Division as grouping

There are 40 strawberries in a punnet. How many people can have 5 each?   40 ÷ 5 =

When grouping, you know how many in each group but not how many groups.

Arranging the strawberries in an array helps to show how many groups.

Division as grouping is just repeated subtraction and arrays!

Draw each group as a jump on the number line to check.

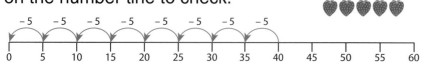

Teacher's Guide

Before working through the *Textbook*, study page 108 of the *Teacher's Guide* to see how the concepts should be introduced. Read and discuss the page with the children. Provide concrete resources to support exploration.

Answer these.

Share the amount to find out how many each. Write the matching division.

a   10 carrots, 5 rabbits.

b   4 sandwiches, 2 children.

c   15 apples, 5 horses.

d   10 stickers, 2 children.

2 **Answer these.**

Put counters into groups to find out how many groups.

a   20 ÷ 2 =

b   20 ÷ 5 =

c   20 ÷ 10 =

d   10 ÷ 2 =

e   25 ÷ 5 =

f   50 ÷ 10 =

3

Measure.

Share these ingredients equally between the 5 mixing bowls.
How much will be in each bowl?
Record as a division calculation.

100 g sugar

50 g butter

5 g salt

10 eggs

500 g flour

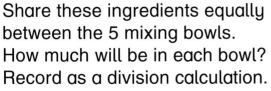

Share these between 2 bowls. How much in each bowl?
Chocolate chips 50 g
Mixed nuts 40 g

4

Investigate.

How many children are in your class today? Could the class be put into groups of 2, 5 or 10, with no one left over each time?

Use counters or number lines to help you. If no one is left over, write the matching division statement.

Teacher's Guide
See page 109 of the *Teacher's Guide* for ideas of how to guide practice.
Work through each step together as a class to develop children's conceptual understanding.

95

5 minute times

Let's learn

It is 5 minutes past 9.

No. The minute hand is pointing at the 5 on the hour scale. It is 25 minutes past 9.

Minutes past

There are 60 minutes in an hour.

The time on this clock is after 7, but not near 8 yet.

The minute hand is pointing to 10 minutes past on the minute scale.

It's 10 minutes after 7 o'clock. It's 10 minutes past 7.

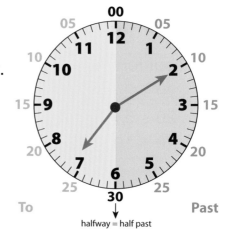

To · Past

halfway = half past

What is the time on this clock?

What time will it be in 5 minutes?

Minutes to

The time on this clock is also after 7, but it is nearly 8 o'clock.

The minute hand is pointing to 20 minutes 'to' on the minutes scale.

It's 20 minutes to 8 o'clock. It's 20 minutes to 8.

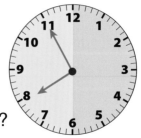

What is the time on this clock?

What time will it be in 5 minutes?

Teacher's Guide

Before working through the *Textbook*, study page 110 of the *Teacher's Guide* to see how the concepts should be introduced. Read and discuss the page with the children. Provide concrete resources to support exploration.

★**96**

1 Answer these.

What is the time?

a

c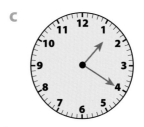

e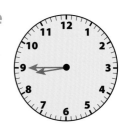

b

d

f

2 Draw.

Draw the hands on a clock face to show each time.

a   15 minutes past 5   c   5 minutes to 3   e   25 minutes to 4

b   25 minutes past 11   d   20 minutes to 12   f   10 minutes past 9

3 Apply.

Roll a dice. The numbers 1 to 6 tell you how many 5 minutes have passed, e.g. 4 is 5 minutes × 4 = 20 minutes. Start at 10 o'clock. Roll the dice and record the new time. Repeat. Can you reach exactly 12 o'clock?

4 Investigate.

Make strip clocks using squared paper.

You need 2 rows of 12 squares. Label the top row 1 to 12 and the bottom row 5 to 60. Colour 1 square on each row to show 20 minutes past 10.

Now show the same time on a strip clock with the top row labelled 0 to 11 and the bottom row 0 to 55.

How are the clocks the same? How are they different?

Teacher's Guide

See page 111 of the *Teacher's Guide* for ideas of how to guide practice. Work through each step together as a class to develop children's conceptual understanding.

97

Cover the clock

Let's play

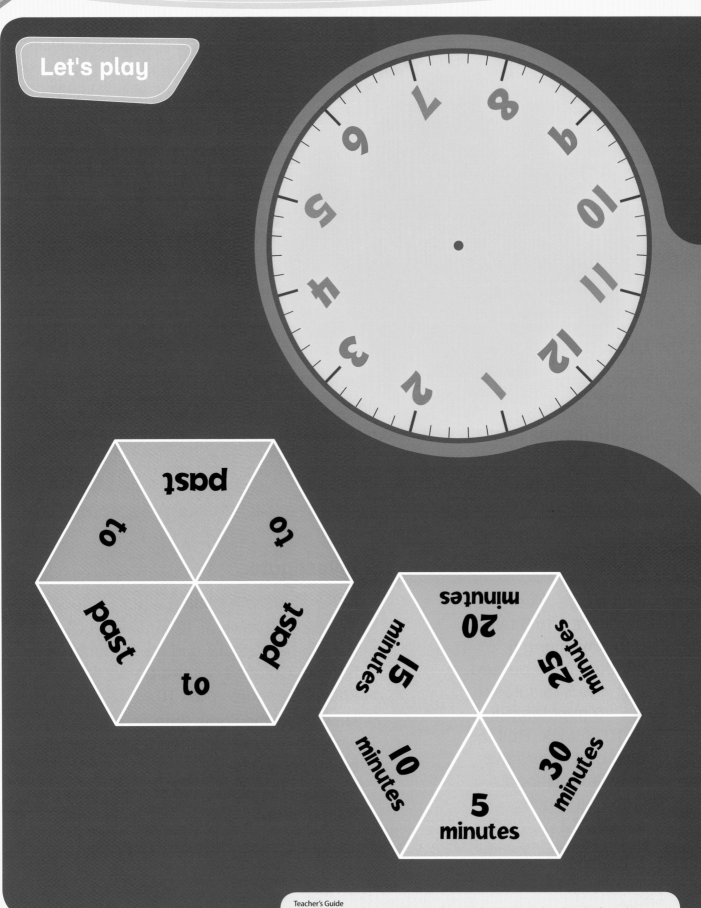

Teacher's Guide

See pages 112–13 of the *Teacher's Guide*. Explain the rules for each game and allow children to choose which to play. Encourage them to challenge themselves and practise what they have learnt in the unit.

1 Past and to

Spin both spinners and be the first to cover the hours' numbers on your clock face.

2 Hours to minutes

Use multiplication table facts for 5 and be the first to cover the hours' numbers with minutes' numbers.

3 Your game

Make up your own game using the gameboard.

And finally ...

1 Tyler and Romesh have forgotten the password for their computer game, but they wrote a code to work it out.

Complete these questions and use the code wheel to find the password.

1   10×3 4 10×7 7 2×12

2   2×9 5 $40 \div 5$ 8 5×9

3   5×5 6 5×6

Choose your own password.

Write multiplication or division clues for each letter.

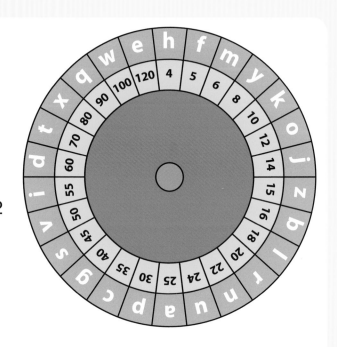

2 Each purse contains only 1 type of coin.

There is 60p in this purse. $10p \times 6 = 60p$. There could be six 10p coins in this purse.

60p

You need:

• 2p, 5p and 10p coins

• 100 square

$10p \times 6 = 60p$

18p   55p   20p

24p   80p

What could be in each purse?

Teacher's Guide
See pages 114–15 of the *Teacher's Guide* for guidance on running each task. Observe children to identify those who have mastered concepts and those who require further consolidation.

 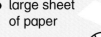

What if you were teaching someone to tell the time?

Make a poster that would help.

Did you know?

The first people to write down multiplication tables were probably the ancient Babylonians. They wrote them on clay tablets This one was found in the desert in Iraq and it is nearly 4000 years old!

What multiplication table fact would you carve into clay to help you remember it?

Parts of a whole

I wonder when and where that was.

What does that mean?

If I ate all the mushroom, how much pizza would I have eaten?

36p

47p

How much is that altogether?

Wow, what is that?

Teacher's Guide
Look at the pictures with the children and discuss the questions.
See pages 116–17 of the *Teacher's Guide* for key ideas to draw out.

103 ★

8a Partitioning to add and subtract (TO and O)

Let's learn

I'm going to partition 8 into 4 and 4 to add it to 48.

It would be easier to partition the 8 into 2 and 6. 48 + 2 is 50, then 50 + 6 is 58.

Partitioning to add

Partition addends to make them easier to add. Look at 37 + 8.

Method 1

Partition 37 into tens and ones.	$37 + 8 = 30 + 7 + 8$
Add the ones.	$30 + 7 + 8 = 30 + 15$
Add them to the tens.	$30 + 15 = 45 \rightarrow 37 + 8 = 45$

Method 2

You know $7 + 3 = 10$.	$37 + 8 = 37 + 3 + 5$
Partition 8 into 3 and 5.	$37 + 3 + 5 = 40 + 5$
Add 37 and 3.	$40 + 5 = 45 \rightarrow 37 + 8 = 45$
Add on the 5.	

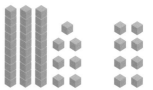

Partitioning to subtract

Partition the minuend to make it easier to subtract from. Look at 45 − 8.

Method 1

You know $10 - 8 = 2$.	$45 - 8 = 35 + 10 - 8$
Partition 45 into 35 and 10.	$35 + 10 - 8 = 35 + 2$
Subtract 8 from the 10.	$35 + 2 = 37 \rightarrow 45 - 8 = 37$
Add 35 and 2.	

Method 2

You cannot subtract 8 from 5, but you can subtract 8 from 15.	
Split 45 into 30 and 15.	$45 - 8 = 30 + 15 - 8$
Subtract 8 from 15.	$30 + 15 - 8 = 30 + 7$
Add 30 and 7.	$30 + 7 = 37 \rightarrow 45 - 8 = 37$

Teacher's Guide

Before working through the *Textbook*, study page 118 of the *Teacher's Guide* to see how the concepts should be introduced. Read and discuss the page with the children. Provide concrete resources to support exploration.

1

Answer these.

Add these numbers. First decide how to partition them.

a   46 + 9   b   57 + 8   c   68 + 7   d   48 + 5   e   77 + 6   f   64 + 7

Choose 2 of the additions.
Can you find the sum another way?

2

Answer these.

Subtract these numbers. First decide how to partition them.

a   53 − 7   b   57 − 8   c   72 − 8   d   73 − 6   e   84 − 9   f   62 − 7

Choose 2 of the subtractions.
Can you find the difference another way?

3

Apply.

Add these amounts.
Use coins to help you partition them.

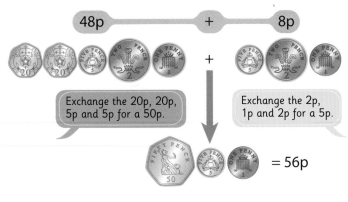

Exchange the 20p, 20p, 5p and 5p for a 50p.

Exchange the 2p, 1p and 2p for a 5p.

= 56p

a   53p + 7p   c   28p + 6p

b   36p + 9p   d   34p + 7p

4

Think.

I think of a number and add 4. The sum is 31. What was my number?

I think of a number and subtract 7. The difference is 43. What was my number?

Write some 'What was my number?' questions.
Test them out on a friend.

Teacher's Guide
See page 119 of the *Teacher's Guide* for ideas of how to guide practice. Work through each step together as a class to develop children's conceptual understanding.

105 ★

Partitioning to add and subtract (TO and TO)

You need:

- number lines
- Base 10 apparatus
- coins 5p 1p 10p

Let's learn

You can only use number bonds for 10 with single-digit numbers.

No, they are just as useful with 2-digit numbers, e.g. you can use 2 + 8 = 10 to help you see that 42 + 8 = 50.

Partitioning to add

Partition augends and addends to make them easier to add. Look at 46 + 37.

Method 1

Partition the augend and addend into tens and ones. Add the tens; add the ones.

$46 + 37 = 40 + 6 + 30 + 7$
$40 + 30 + 6 + 7 = 70 + 13$
$70 + 13 = 83 \rightarrow 46 + 37 = 83$

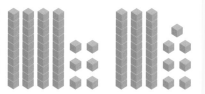

Method 2

You know that 6 + 4 = 10.
Partition 37 into 33 and 4.
Add 46 and 4.
Then add on 33.

$46 + 37 = 46 + 33 + 4$
$46 + 33 + 4 = 50 + 33$
$50 + 33 = 83 \rightarrow 46 + 37 = 83$

Partitioning to subtract

Partition the minuend to make it easier to subtract from. Look at 65 − 48.

Method 1

Split 65 into 50 and 15.
Subtract 48 from 50.
Add 2 and 15.

$65 - 48 = 50 + 15 - 48$
$50 + 15 - 48 = 2 + 15$
$2 + 15 = 17 \rightarrow 65 - 48 = 17$

Method 2

You cannot subtract 8 from 5, but you can subtract 8 from 15. Split 65 into 50 and 15. Split 48 into 40 and 8. Subtract 40 from 50. Subtract 8 from 15. Add 10 and 7.

$65 - 48 = 50 + 15 - 40 - 8$
$50 + 15 - 40 - 8 = 10 + 7$
$10 + 7 = 17 \rightarrow 65 - 48 = 17$

Teacher's Guide

Before working through the *Textbook*, study page 120 of the *Teacher's Guide* to see how the concepts should be introduced. Read and discuss the page with the children. Provide concrete resources to support exploration.

1

Answer these.

Add these numbers.
First decide how to partition them.
Choose 2 of the additions.
Can you find the sum another way?

a 46 + 29

b 57 + 35

c 68 + 17

d 48 + 25

e 37 + 26

f 62 + 37

2

Answer these.

Subtract these numbers.
First decide how to partition them.

a 53 − 27

b 57 − 28

c 72 − 48

d 73 − 36

e 84 − 39

f 82 − 47

3

Solve.

How much is your change from
£1 if you buy each fruit?

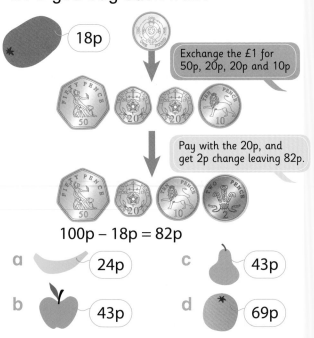

Exchange the £1 for
50p, 20p, 20p and 10p

Pay with the 20p, and
get 2p change leaving 82p.

100p − 18p = 82p

a 24p

b 43p

c 43p

d 69p

4

Investigate.

Copy the addition pyramid.
Choose 3 different numbers
between 10 and 20.
Write them in the bottom row.
Add the 2 numbers next to
each other. Write the total in
the box above.
What is the greatest sum
you can make at the top of
the pyramid? What is the
least sum?

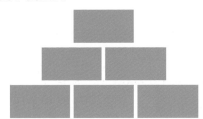

Teacher's Guide

See page 121 of the *Teacher's Guide* for ideas of how to guide practice.
Work through each step together as a class to develop children's
conceptual understanding.

107 ★

Fractions of a whole

You need:

- squared paper
- ruler
- ribbon
- scissors

Let's learn

Fractions aren't really numbers. They are just a way of labelling parts of the whole.

Fractions are numbers too! Halfway between zero and 1 on the number line is a half.

Half and double

Halving is the same as dividing by 2.

Doubling is the same as multiplying by 2.

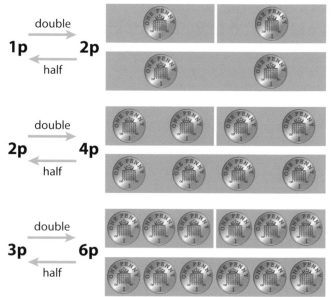

double
1p → 2p
← half

double
2p → 4p
← half

double
3p → 6p
← half

Halves and quarters

A half is 1 of 2 equal parts of a whole.

A quarter is 1 of 4 equal parts of a whole.

| 1 |

| $\frac{1}{2}$ | $\frac{1}{2}$ | 1 half = 2 quarters $\frac{1}{2} = \frac{2}{4}$

| $\frac{1}{4}$ | $\frac{1}{4}$ | $\frac{1}{4}$ | $\frac{1}{4}$ | 2 halves = 4 quarters. $\frac{2}{2} = \frac{4}{4}$

| $\frac{1}{4}$ | $\frac{1}{4}$ | $\frac{1}{4}$ | 3 quarters is written $\frac{3}{4}$

You write fractions like this:

1 The numerator tells you how many parts you have.

— The line in between is called the vinculum.

4 The denominator tells you how many equal parts the whole is divided into.

Teacher's Guide

Before working through the *Textbook*, study page 122 of the *Teacher's Guide* to see how the concepts should be introduced. Read and discuss the page with the children. Provide concrete resources to support exploration.

Let's practise

1 Answer this.

Copy and complete the grid.
Continue to at least 10.

1	double → ← half	2
2	double → ← half	4
	double → ← half	6
	double → ← half	8

Describe the pattern of the doubles numbers.

2 Answer these.

What fraction of each shape is shaded in green?

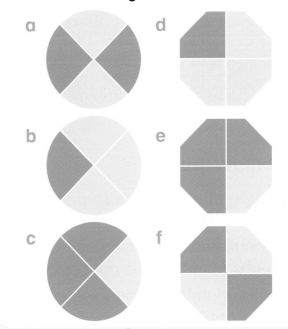

3 Apply.

Cut 3 lengths of ribbon or string: 12 cm, 16 cm and 20 cm.
Find $\frac{1}{4}$, $\frac{2}{4}$ and $\frac{3}{4}$ of each length.
Record the lengths in a table.

Whole length	12 cm	16 cm	20 cm
$\frac{1}{4}$ length			
$\frac{2}{4}$ length			
$\frac{3}{4}$ length			

Is $\frac{1}{2}$ the same as $\frac{2}{4}$?
How do you know?

4 Think.

a   I have less than 50p but more than 30p.
A quarter and three-quarters of my money are odd numbers. How much could I have?

b   A piece of string is more than 50 cm long but less than a metre.
A quarter and three-quarters of the length are even numbers. How long could the string be?

Teacher's Guide

See page 123 of the *Teacher's Guide* for ideas of how to guide practice.
Work through each step together as a class to develop children's conceptual understanding.

109

Let's learn

It's hot today, I'm boiling! It must be at least 100°C.

It's 28°C today. When you boil the kettle, the water is 100°C. It would have to be 72 degrees hotter to really be boiling!

Temperature

Temperature is measured in degrees Celsius (°C).

A small number of degrees Celsius means something is cool or cold.

Higher numbers mean something is warm or hot.

Measuring temperature

You measure temperature with a thermometer.

A thermometer scale is like a number line.

The scale on this thermometer is marked in ones.

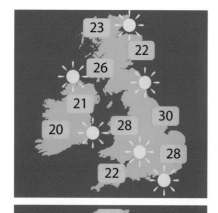

Summer

Winter

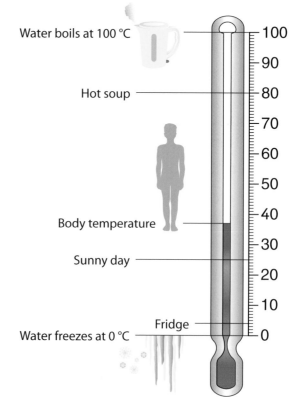

Water boils at 100 °C

Hot soup

Body temperature

Sunny day

Fridge

Water freezes at 0 °C

Teacher's Guide

Before working through the *Textbook*, study page 124 of the *Teacher's Guide* to see how the concepts should be introduced. Read and discuss the page with the children. Provide concrete resources to support exploration.

1

Record.

Write down these temperatures.

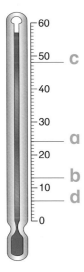

What would each temperature be if it was 8 °C warmer?

2

Record.

Write down these temperatures.

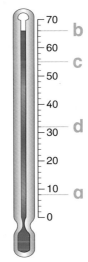

What would each temperature be if it was 6 °C cooler?

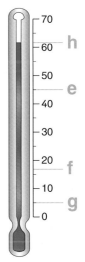

What would each temperature be if it was 15 °C hotter?

3

Draw.

Day	Monday	Tuesday	Wednesday	Thursday	Friday	Saturday	Sunday
Temperature	16 °C	13 °C	17 °C	18 °C	14 °C	12 °C	11 °C

Draw a block diagram of the week's temperatures. Write two < and > statements about the temperatures, e.g. Thursday 18 °C > Sunday 11 °C.

4

Think.

Write 6 questions which can be answered from the table or block diagram in Step 3.

Which day was the warmest?

What was the temperature on the warmest day?

Teacher's Guide

See page 125 of the *Teacher's Guide* for ideas of how to guide practice. Work through each step together as a class to develop children's conceptual understanding.

111

Boil the kettle!

Let's play

Teacher's Guide

See pages 126–7 of the *Teacher's Guide*. Explain the rules for each game and allow children to choose which to play. Encourage them to challenge themselves and practise what they have learnt in the unit.

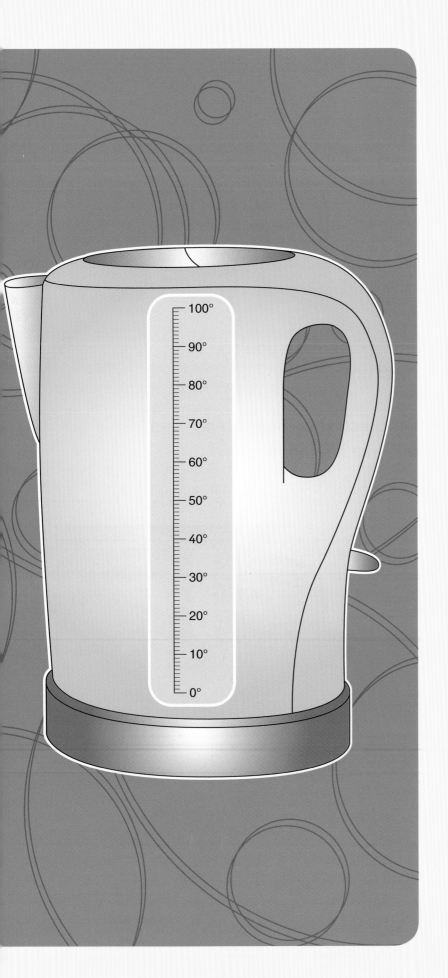

1 **Hotter and hotter**

Race up the thermometer to make the kettle boil at 100 °C!

2 **Power cuts**

Can you make your kettle boil despite power cuts?

3 **Your game**

Make up your own game using the gameboard.

Let's review

1 Choose any 2 of these numbers.
Find the sum by partitioning and regrouping.
Then subtract them to find the difference.

18 29 37 46

What is the largest sum and the largest difference you can find?
How much larger than the next largest are they?

What is the smallest sum and the smallest difference you can find?
How much smaller than the next smallest are they?

2 Class 2M took the temperature in the playground at 11 o'clock every day for a week.

14°C 16°C 18°C 19°C 22°C

The temperature on Tuesday was halfway between the temperature on Monday and Wednesday.
The lowest temperature was on Wednesday.
The highest temperature was on Monday.
It was warmer on Friday than on Tuesday.

Draw a grid to show the temperatures for each day.

Teacher's Guide

See pages 128–9 of the *Teacher's Guide* for guidance on running each task.
Observe children to identify those who have mastered concepts and those who require further consolidation.

★114

a Louis eats a quarter of a bar of chocolate. His brother Sam eats half of what is left. Who eats more? How much is left?

b Which fractions have the same value? Write some number statements comparing these fractions.

Remember:
< means 'is less than'
= means 'is equivalent to'
> means ' is greater than'

c Sally counted in quarters from 0. Write the rest of her count to 5.

$0, \frac{1}{4}, \frac{2}{4}, \frac{3}{4}, 1, 1\frac{1}{4} ...$

d George counted in halves from 0. Write the rest of his count to 5.

$0, \frac{1}{2}, 1, 1\frac{1}{2}, 2 ...$

Did you know?

Every whole number can also be written as a fraction.

We can write the number 1 as $\frac{1}{1}$, or 1 oneth. So 2 would be $\frac{2}{1}$, 2 oneths, 2 divided into 1 equal piece. 3 would be $\frac{3}{1}$, 3 oneths, and so on!

$$\frac{1}{1} \quad \frac{2}{1} \quad \frac{3}{1} \quad \frac{4}{1} \quad \frac{5}{1} \quad \frac{6}{1} \quad \frac{7}{1} \quad \frac{8}{1} \quad \frac{9}{1}$$

More addition and subtraction

I wonder if all new coins have the amount in words, not numbers?

How I can find out how much fruit there is altogether?

12
tennis balls

3 free

If 3 are free, how many do you pay for?

I wonder how many pencils there are altogether?

36 coloured pencils

20

80 lights
Christmas
~~**Lights**~~

7 lights broken

How many lights are still working?

Teacher's Guide

Look at the pictures with the children and discuss the questions.
See pages 130–1 of the *Teacher's Guide* for key ideas to draw out.

117 ★

You need:

- Base 10 apparatus
- number line
- place-value cards 4 9
- bead strings

Let's learn

You have to partition both numbers if you are adding or subtracting two 2-digit numbers.

That's useful at first, but you can keep the first number whole, then add or subtract tens then ones.

Adding by sequencing

To add two 2-digit numbers, keep the augend whole and only partition the addend. This is called sequencing.

Use a number line to help or add mentally.

$$35 + 28 = 35 + 20 + 8$$
$$= 55 + 8$$
$$= 63$$

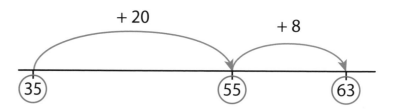

Add 8 any way you choose.

You could add 5 then 3. You could add 10 and take away 2.

Subtracting by sequencing

To subtract, keep the minuend whole and just partition the subtrahend.

Use a number line to help or subtract mentally.

$$67 - 34 = 67 - 30 - 4$$
$$= 37 - 4$$
$$= 33$$

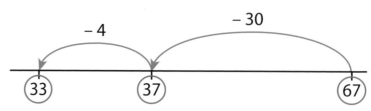

Subtract 4 any way you choose.

Teacher's Guide

Before working through the *Textbook*, study page 132 of the *Teacher's Guide* to see how the concepts should be introduced. Read and discuss the page with the children. Provide concrete resources to support exploration.

★ **118**

1 Calculate.

Use sequencing to complete each number statement.

a 67 + 26 = c 28 + 55 = e 83 − 48 =

b 48 + 37 = d 59 − 45 = f 74 − 36 =

Record what you did on a number line.

2 Calculate.

Use a number line or Base 10 apparatus to help you.

What do you need to add to or subtract from each of these numbers to reach a total of 57?

a 28 c 44 e 89

b 32 d 72 f 95

3 Apply.

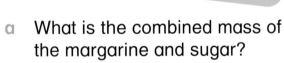

Mini shortbread biscuits recipe

55 g flour
26 g margarine
18 g sugar
Milk to mix

a What is the combined mass of the margarine and sugar?

b The flour is added to the margarine and sugar. What is the mass of the ingredients now?

c 10 grams of milk is added to mixture. What is the total mass of the ingredients now?

4 Think.

11	12	13	14
21	22	23	24
31	32	33	34
41	42	43	44

Choose a number from the grid. Write it down.

Swap the digits. Write down the new number.

Add the two 2-digit numbers together.

What do you notice?

Choose different numbers. Does the same thing happen?

Teacher's Guide
See page 133 of the *Teacher's Guide* for ideas of how to guide practice. Work through each step together as a class to develop children's conceptual understanding.

119

Adding and subtracting a near multiple of 10

Let's learn

To subtract 19, I subtract 20 then subtract 1 more because 20 is 1 more than 19.

Then you have subtracted 21! You need to subtract 20 then add 1 back.

Adding a near multiple of 10

To add a near multiple of 10, add the multiple of 10 and adjust.

$57 + 28$

28 is close to 30. Add 30 then subtract 2 because you added 2 too many.

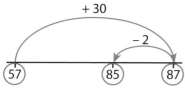

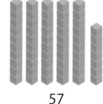

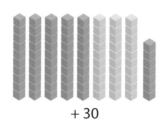

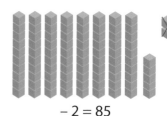

57       $+ 30$ $- 2 = 85$

If the number is a little more than a multiple of 10 use sequencing.

Subtracting a near multiple of 10

To subtract a near multiple of 10, subtract the multiple of 10 and adjust.

$57 - 28$

28 is near to 30. Subtract 30 then add back 2 because you subtracted 2 too many.

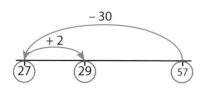

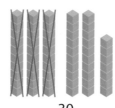

57       $- 30$ $+ 2 = 29$

If the number is a little more than a multiple of 10 use sequencing.

Teacher's Guide

Before working through the *Textbook*, study page 134 of the *Teacher's Guide* to see how the concepts should be introduced. Read and discuss the page with the children. Provide concrete resources to support exploration.

★ 120

Let's practise

1 Calculate.

Complete each number statement. Add or subtract a multiple of 10 and adjust.

Record what you did on a number line.

a   36 + 27   c   36 + 29   e   74 – 38

b   36 + 28   d   74 – 37   f   74 – 39

2 Answer these.

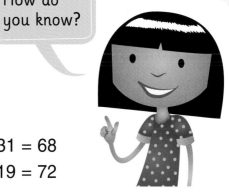

How do you know?

Are these number statements true or false?

Check using a number line, Base 10 apparatus or something else.

a   98 – 18 = 60   c   82 – 27 = 65   e   27 + 31 = 68

b   75 – 19 = 56   d   44 + 28 = 82   f   53 + 19 = 72

3 Apply.

Seb buys a 1 metre liquorice shoelace on Monday.

Copy and complete the table to show how much he eats each day.

Day	Eaten today	Left at end of day
Monday	29 cm	
Tuesday	18 cm	
Wednesday	15 cm	
Thursday	17 cm	
Friday	?	0

4 Think.

Choose and write down a number from the grid.

57	58	59	14
67	68	69	24
77	78	79	34
87	88	89	44
97	98	99	44

Swap the digits. Write that number.

Subtract the smaller number from the larger number.

What do you notice?

Teacher's Guide

See page 135 of the *Teacher's Guide* for ideas of how to guide practice. Work through each step together as a class to develop children's conceptual understanding.

121 ★

Numbers in words

Let's learn

You can write numbers to 10 in words, but you just write the rest in numbers.

That's not true! Any number can be written in words.

You need:
- place-value cards 4 9

Numbers in words to 100

You can write numbers in words as well as in numerals.

0	zero	10	ten	20	twenty
1	one	11	eleven	30	thirty
2	two	12	twelve	40	forty
3	three	13	thirteen	50	fifty
4	four	14	fourteen	60	sixty
5	five	15	fifteen	70	seventy
6	six	16	sixteen	80	eighty
7	seven	17	seventeen	90	ninety
8	eight	18	eighteen	100	one hundred
9	nine	19	nineteen		

Make a number using place-value cards. Separate the cards and write each part.

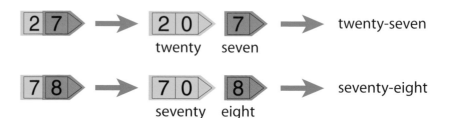

Numbers in words beyond 100

To write a number over 100, you need the word **and** as well as **hundred**.
Make a number using place-value cards. Separate the cards and write each part.

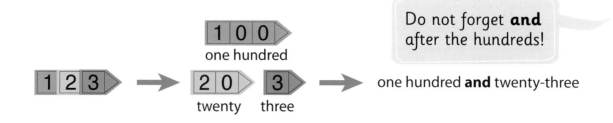

Do not forget **and** after the hundreds!

Teacher's Guide

Before working through the *Textbook*, study page 136 of the *Teacher's Guide* to see how the concepts should be introduced. Read and discuss the page with the children. Provide concrete resources to support exploration.

Let's practise

1 Write.

Write these numbers in numerals.

a forty-seven

b fifty-seven

c one hundred and sixty-seven

d eighty-three

e eighty-four

2 Write.

Use these number words to make as many 2-digit numbers as you can.

thirty	fifty	seventy
four	six	eight

3 Apply.

Write each distance in words.
These are in kilometres.

a	Las Vegas	72
b	Salt Lake City	193
c	New York	230

These are in metres.

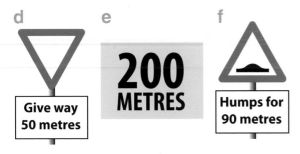

d Give way 50 metres

e 200 METRES

f Humps for 90 metres

4 Think.

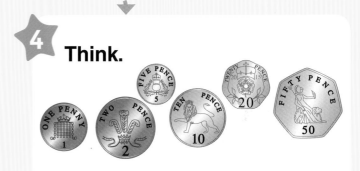

Which 3 coins make each of these totals? You can use any coin more than once.

a seventeen pence

b twenty-two pence

c sixty-five pence

d thirty-one pence

Find 3 other amounts between 50p and 100p which can be made using 3 coins.

Write the values in words.

Teacher's Guide
See page 137 of the *Teacher's Guide* for ideas of how to guide practice. Work through each step together as a class to develop children's conceptual understanding.

123 ★

Upstairs, downstairs

Let's play

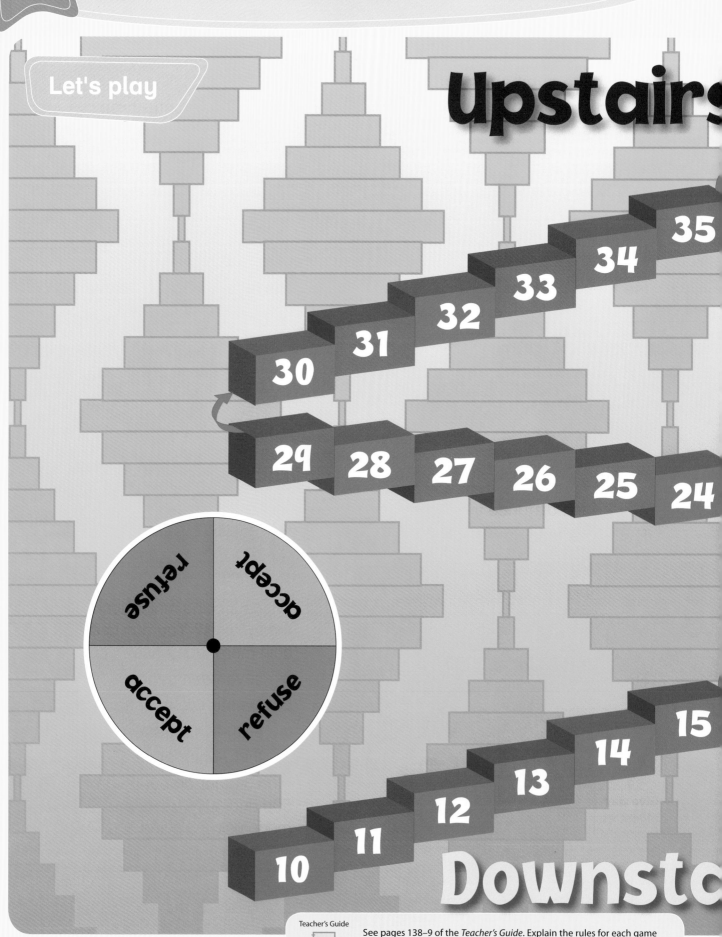

Upstairs

35 34 33 32 31 30

29 28 27 26 25 24

refuse accept
accept refuse

15 14 13 12 11 10

Downsto

Teacher's Guide

See pages 138–9 of the *Teacher's Guide*. Explain the rules for each game and allow children to choose which to play. Encourage them to challenge themselves and practise what they have learnt in the unit.

1 **Upstairs**

Collect the numbers on the stairs, adding them until you get upstairs.

2 **Downstairs**

Subtract the number you land on from 100. Keep subtracting until you get downstairs.

3 **Your game**

Make up your own game using the gameboard. Explain the rules and play with a partner.

And finally ...

Let's review

1 Use place-value cards to make nine 2-digit numbers.

a Put them in order from smallest to greatest.
b Add 18 to the 4 smallest numbers.
c Subtract 27 from the 5 largest numbers.
d Order your new numbers from greatest to smallest.

You need:
- place-value cards (tens and ones) 4 9

Add or subtract a multiple of 10 and adjust.

2 A new box of 100 teabags is opened on Monday morning.

The table shows how many teabags are used each day.

How many are used on Friday so that none are left in the box?

You need:
- place-value cards (tens and ones) 4 9

Day	Teabags used today	Teabags left at end of day
Monday	18	
Tuesday	19	
Wednesday	27	
Thursday	17	
Friday	?	0

Copy and complete the table. Use sequencing to help you.

Teacher's Guide

See pages 140–1 of the *Teacher's Guide* for guidance on running each task. Observe children to identify those who have mastered concepts and those who require further consolidation.

3 All bus numbers in Wordtown are written in words.

a Shuffle your digit cards.

Lay them out in five pairs to make five 2-digit bus numbers.

Write each bus number in words.

b There are so many buses that there are now some 3-digit bus numbers!

Shuffle your digit cards.

Lay out 3 sets of 3 numbers to make three 3-digit bus numbers.

Write each bus number in words.

Which digit did you have left over?

Write that number in words too.

Did you know?

The words eleven and twelve come from Old English. They mean 'one left over after ten' and 'two left over after ten'.

Seconteen tennis balls

Some people think eleven and twelve should be renamed firsteen and seconteen. What do you think?

Exploring shapes

What is the same and what is different?

How would you describe the pattern on the pineapple's skin?

What is special about this carpet?

I wonder what would happen if you used cuboids for the wheels?

I wonder how many different shapes were used to make this toy?

Teacher's Guide
Look at the pictures with the children and discuss the questions.
See pages 142–3 of the *Teacher's Guide* for key ideas to draw out.

129 ★

Exploring faces

Let's learn

I think these are prisms.

That's not right! A prism is a 3-D shape with 2 ends the same and only flat sides. The second shape is not a prism.

Pyramids and prisms

Name	Square-based pyramid	Triangular prism
Number of faces	5	5
Number of triangular faces	4	2
Number of rectangular faces	1	3

Grouping 3-D shapes

You can group 3-D shapes according to their faces.

These shapes have flat, rectangular faces.

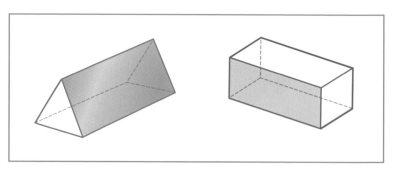

These shapes have curved surfaces and 1 or 2 circular faces.

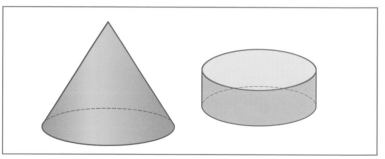

Teacher's Guide

Before working through the *Textbook*, study page 144 of the *Teacher's Guide* to see how the concepts should be introduced. Read and discuss the page with the children. Provide concrete resources to support exploration.

1

Answer this. Which shape is the odd one out? Why?

a   b   c   d   e   f

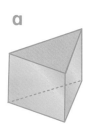 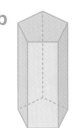 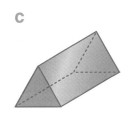 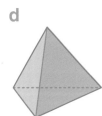 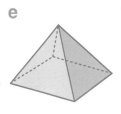 

2

Sort.

What shape is each object?

Objects with rectangular faces		Objects with fewer than 10 vertices

Can you think of another way to group them?

3

Make.

Use these shapes to create 2 different structures.

Write down the shapes you used.

Count the faces on your structure and compare with the faces of each shape. What do you notice?

4

Investigate.

Look at these 2-D shapes.

They could all be faces on 3-D shapes.

Which 3-D shapes could they belong to?

a    c

b   d

Teacher's Guide

See page 145 of the *Teacher's Guide* for ideas of how to guide practice. Work through each step together as a class to develop children's conceptual understanding.

131 ★

Let's learn

You need:

- 2-D shapes
- 3-D shapes
- tangrams

I can only make 1 shape with these triangles — a square.

No, there are more. I can make another triangle! What else can you make?

Tessellation

Tessellation is a pattern of flat shapes that do not overlap or have gaps. They cover a surface.

This design is made by using triangles.

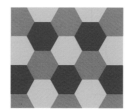

This design is made by using hexagons.

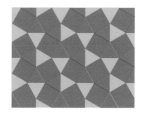

Do you think there are more squares or triangles in this pattern?

Art with shapes

Shapes are used in different ways.

How were this cat and tiger made?

Which shapes can you see?

How many sides has each shape?

How many shapes are there altogether?

Teacher's Guide

Before working through the *Textbook*, study page 146 of the *Teacher's Guide* to see how the concepts should be introduced. Read and discuss the page with the children. Provide concrete resources to support exploration.

1 Answer this.

These shapes fit perfectly together.

If you had lots of 1 kind of these shapes, which would fit perfectly together with no gaps?

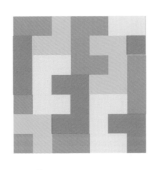

a b c  d e f

2 Make.

a How many triangles can you use to make a larger triangle?

b How many rectangles can you use to make a larger rectangle?

Now make these shapes using tangrams. How many shapes did you use?

I can make different shapes using these 2 shapes.

c  d

3 Design.

Look at the artworks on page 132.

Make your own artwork using:

a squares only

b triangles only

4 Investigate.

Cut a square in 2 parts. Glue the parts next to each other on a sheet of paper.

Cut out the new shape and draw around it.

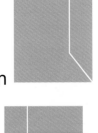

Create a pattern of new shapes next to each other.

Teacher's Guide   See page 147 of the *Teacher's Guide* for ideas of how to guide practice. Work through each step together as a class to develop children's conceptual understanding.

133 ⭐

I spy ... a shape!

Let's play

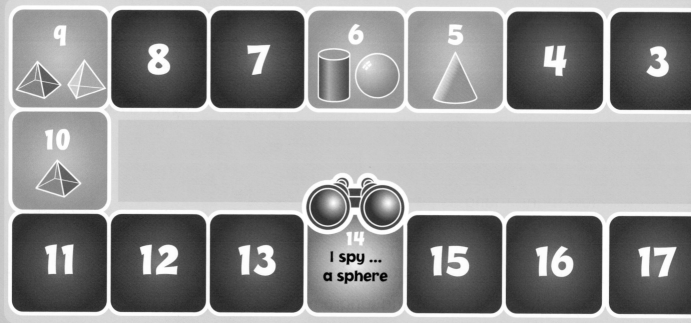

Teacher's Guide

See pages 148–9 of the *Teacher's Guide*. Explain the rules for each game and allow children to choose which to play. Encourage them to challenge themselves and practise what they have learnt in the unit.

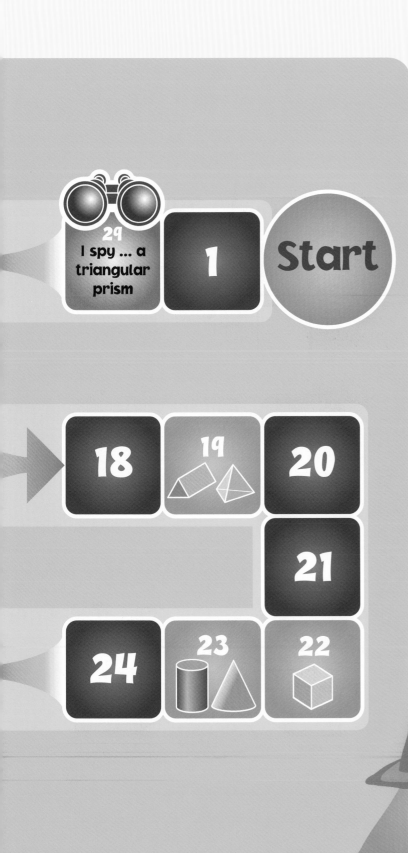

29
I spy ... a triangular prism

1

Start

18

19

20

21

24

23

22

⭐ 1 Who am I?
Name and describe the shapes to collect points. Who will get the most points?

⭐ 2 Shape faces
Identify the 2-D shape faces of the 3-D shapes. Collect points as you go. Who will be the winner?

⭐ 3 Your game
Make up your own game using the gameboard. Explain the rules and play with a partner.

135⭐

And finally ...

Let's review

1

Look at the picture.

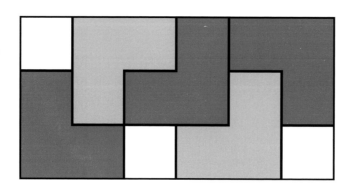

What is wrong?
How can you correct it?

You need:

- 6 L-shapes made from squares
- square grid

Can you make a different pattern using the 6 L-shapes?

2

All prisms have 6 faces. All pyramids have 5 faces.

You need:

- 3-D shapes including triangular prisms and pyramids.

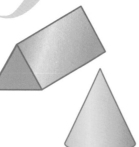

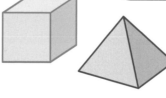

Is Lili correct?
Find shapes to prove your answer. Describe their properties.

Not all shapes are either prisms or pyramids!

Teacher's Guide

See pages 150–1 of the *Teacher's Guide* for guidance on running each task. Observe children to identify those who have mastered concepts and those who require further consolidation.

3

Work in a small group. Look at these pairs of shapes.

Compare the shapes in each pair.

Write 3 statements that are false when you compare them.

 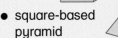 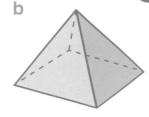
a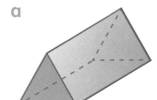

b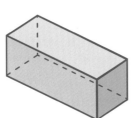

Now change the false statements to make them true.

 What 2-D shapes can you see?

What 2-D shapes can you *not* see?

Did you know?

Some farmers in Japan grow watermelons with flat faces, rather than curved ones. They are easier to put in the fridge and don't roll around. They grow them in glass pots in the shape of cubes.

What shape is your favourite fruit?

What time
is it?

What time will
the shop be
open?

I wonder what
the 1 means?

Teacher's Guide
Look at the pictures with the children and discuss the questions.
See pages 152–3 of the *Teacher's Guide* for key ideas to draw out.

139 ⭐

Millilitres

Let's learn

I emptied the carton of orange juice this morning; I drank a whole litre.

The carton wasn't full, so it couldn't have been a whole litre. You just drank lots of millilitres.

Measuring in millilitres

To measure millilitres you use a measuring cylinder.

Read the scale to find out how many millilitres it contains.

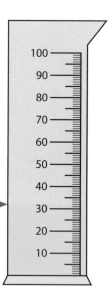

Scale marked in ones: 32 ml

Scale marked in fives: 32 ml

Tables

You can use tables to sort and display information.

This table shows how much rain fell on a school playground each day for 2 weeks.

The largest number in the table is 11.

11 ml of rain fell on Tuesday of week 2.

This was the greatest rainfall in these 2 weeks.

Day	Rainfall, ml	
	Week 1	Week 2
Monday	0	4
Tuesday	3	11
Wednesday	0	0
Thursday	0	0
Friday	7	0
Saturday	2	4
Sunday	1	3

It did not rain on 6 of the days. A zero is written in the table for those days.

3 ml of rain fell on 2 days, Tuesday in week 1 and Sunday in week 2.

Teacher's Guide

Before working through the *Textbook*, study page 154 of the *Teacher's Guide* to see how the concepts should be introduced. Read and discuss the page with the children. Provide concrete resources to support exploration.

⭐ **140**

1 Answer these.

How many millilitres are in each measuring cylinder?

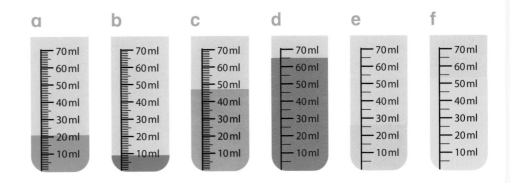

a   b   c   d   e   f

2 Answer these.

a   Order the amounts in Step 1 from smallest to greatest.

b   Write 4 number statements comparing the amounts, e.g. 21 ml < 53 ml.

c   Find 2 amounts in Step 1 that can be added together to give another amount in Step 1.

Remember:
< means 'is less than'
> means 'is greater than'

3 Apply.

Which 2 liquids from Step 1 can the scientist mix to make exactly 120 ml?

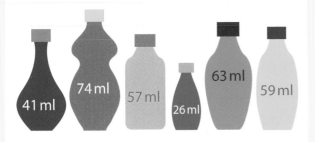

41 ml   74 ml   57 ml   26 ml   63 ml   59 ml

4 Think.

Three lots of 330 ml cans are a little less than 1 litre.

Cans come in packs of 6, 12, 15 and 24.

a   Find 3 different ways to get 10 litres of fizzy drink.

b   Two cans cost £1. How much does each pack cost?

Teacher's Guide

See page 155 of the *Teacher's Guide* for ideas of how to guide practice. Work through each step together as a class to develop children's conceptual understanding.

141

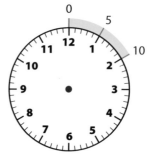
Let's learn

It's only 25 past 11. It's hours until lunchtime at 15 minutes past 12.

It's not even 1 hour! There are 35 minutes until 12 o'clock and 15 minutes after 12 o'clock. That's 50 minutes altogether.

Finding time intervals

How long is the lesson?

Maths starts   Maths ends

Method 1

Count in fives from the 3 to the 12. There are 45 minutes to 10 o'clock.

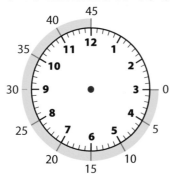

Count in fives from 10 o'clock to 10 past 10. There are 10 minutes.

The total lesson time is 45 mins + 10 mins = 55 mins.

Method 1

You could also use the fact that there are 60 minutes in an hour.

Quarter past 9 is 15 minutes past 9.

60 − 15 = 45, so there are 45 minutes to the next hour.

10 past 10 means 10 minutes have passed since the hour.

The total lesson time is 45 mins + 10 mins = 55 mins.

Teacher's Guide

Before working through the *Textbook*, study page 156 of the *Teacher's Guide* to see how the concepts should be introduced. Read and discuss the page with the children. Provide concrete resources to support exploration.

1 Answer these.

How long is each lesson?

a   Science starts   ends   c   PE starts   ends

 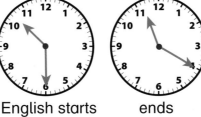  

b   English starts   ends   d   Reading starts   ends

2 Answer these.

a   A lesson starts at quarter past 9. It lasts 35 minutes.
    What time will it finish?

b   What if the lesson started at these times? What time would it finish?

       10 past 10   20 to 11   10 to 12

3 Solve.

How long is your school day? How much of that time are you in lessons?

Use your class timetable and a clock to help you.

4 Think.

Design a timetable for your perfect school day.

How long will you spend doing each activity?

What will you spend the most and least time doing?

Breaks and lunch must be at the same time as they are today.

Teacher's Guide

See page 157 of the *Teacher's Guide* for ideas of how to guide practice.
Work through each step together as a class to develop children's
conceptual understanding.

143

Let's learn

When mum cuts a pizza into thirds, my sister always chooses the big third.

There shouldn't be a big third. A third is 1 of 3 equal parts of a whole. All 3 thirds must be the same size.

Thirds

A third is 1 of 3 equal parts of a whole. The whole can be a length, shape, set of objects or quantity.

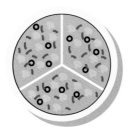

The numerator shows how many parts you have.

The denominator shows how many parts the whole is divided into.

$\frac{1}{3}$

To find $\frac{1}{3}$ of something, divide the whole into 3 equal parts.

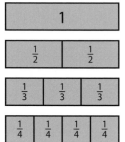

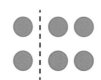 $\frac{1}{3}$ of 6 = 2

10 cm 20 cm 30 cm

$\frac{1}{3}$ of 30 cm = 10 cm

Other thirds

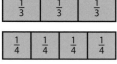

September 2016

SUNDAY	MONDAY	TUESDAY	WEDNESDAY	THURSDAY	FRIDAY	SATURDAY
				1	2	③	4	5	6
7	8	9	10	11	12	13
14	15	16	17	18	19	20
21	22	23	24	25	26	27
28	29	30				

First Second Third

Painting Competition!
1st prize
2nd prize
3rd prize
★ Entries in by 23rd August

Teacher's Guide

Before working through the *Textbook*, study page 158 of the *Teacher's Guide* to see how the concepts should be introduced. Read and discuss the page with the children. Provide concrete resources to support exploration.

1 Find.

Cut a square of paper, 9 squares by 9 squares.
There are 81 squares altogether.

Fold it and cut it into thirds.

Copy and complete this statement: $\frac{1}{3}$ of 81 = [ ] .

Find and record $\frac{1}{3}$ of each new third until only 1 square is left.

2 Find.

Find $\frac{1}{3}$ of each of these.

a   a pack of 12 sweets   d   18 cm   f   a bunch of
b   24 apples   e   3 m   9 bananas
c   6 kg   g   15 pencils

Record your answers like this: $\frac{1}{3}$ of [ ] = [ ]

3 Design.

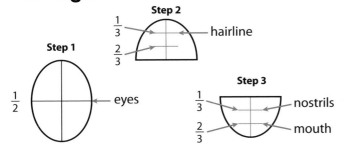

Step 1
$\frac{1}{2}$ ← eyes

Step 2
$\frac{1}{3}$
$\frac{2}{3}$ ← hairline

Step 3
$\frac{1}{3}$ ← nostrils
$\frac{2}{3}$ ← mouth

a   Fold a paper oval in half down
    the middle. Fold in quarters by
    folding across.

b   Add the features shown in
    steps 2 and 3. Make the face
    look like you!

4 Investigate.

a   Use coins to help you
    find $\frac{1}{3}$ of each amount
    of money.
    6p   30p   15p
    21p   9p   60p
    Record each answer
    as $\frac{1}{3}$ of [ ] p = [ ] p

b   Which $\frac{1}{3}$ amounts can
    you make with exactly
    3 coins? Which coins
    will you need?

Teacher's Guide
See page 159 of the *Teacher's Guide* for ideas of how to guide practice.
Work through each step together as a class to develop children's
conceptual understanding.

Game board 11

Liquid gold

Let's play

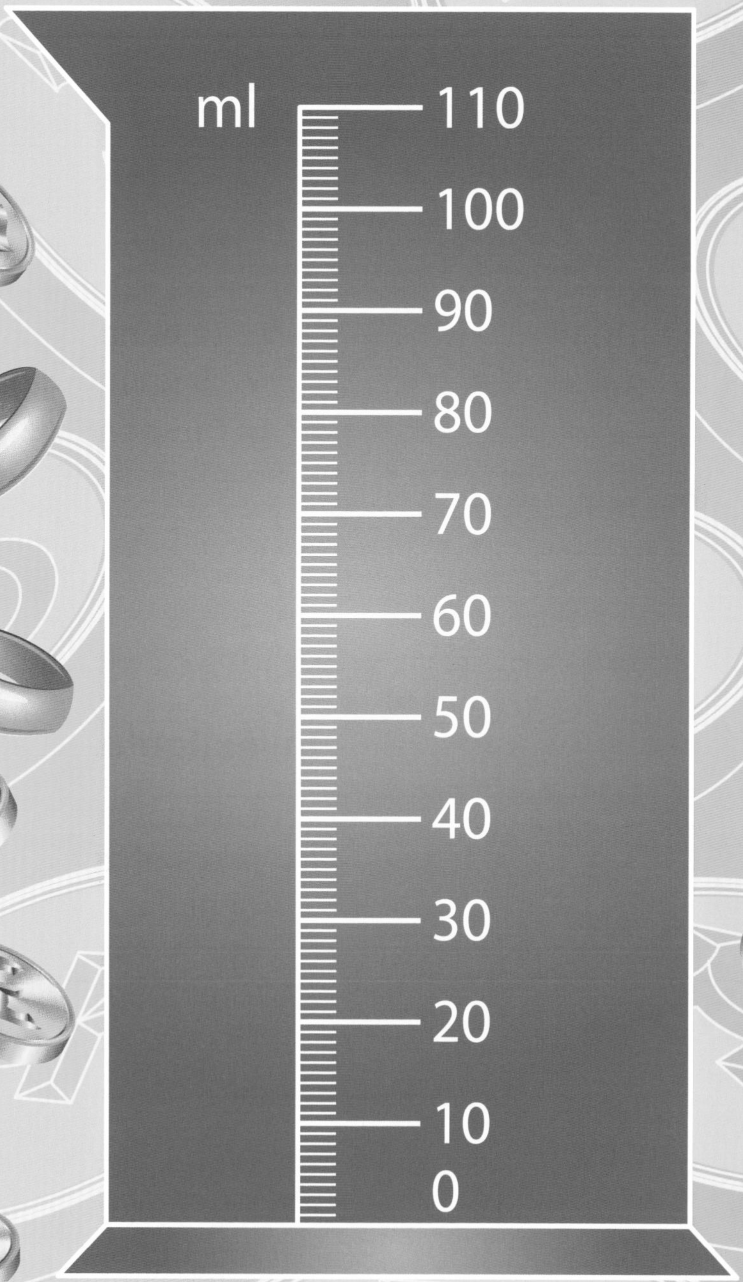
ml
110
100
90
80
70
60
50
40
30
20
10
0

Teacher's Guide

See pages 160–1 of the *Teacher's Guide*. Explain the rules for each game and allow children to choose which to play. Encourage them to challenge themselves and practise what they have learnt in the unit.

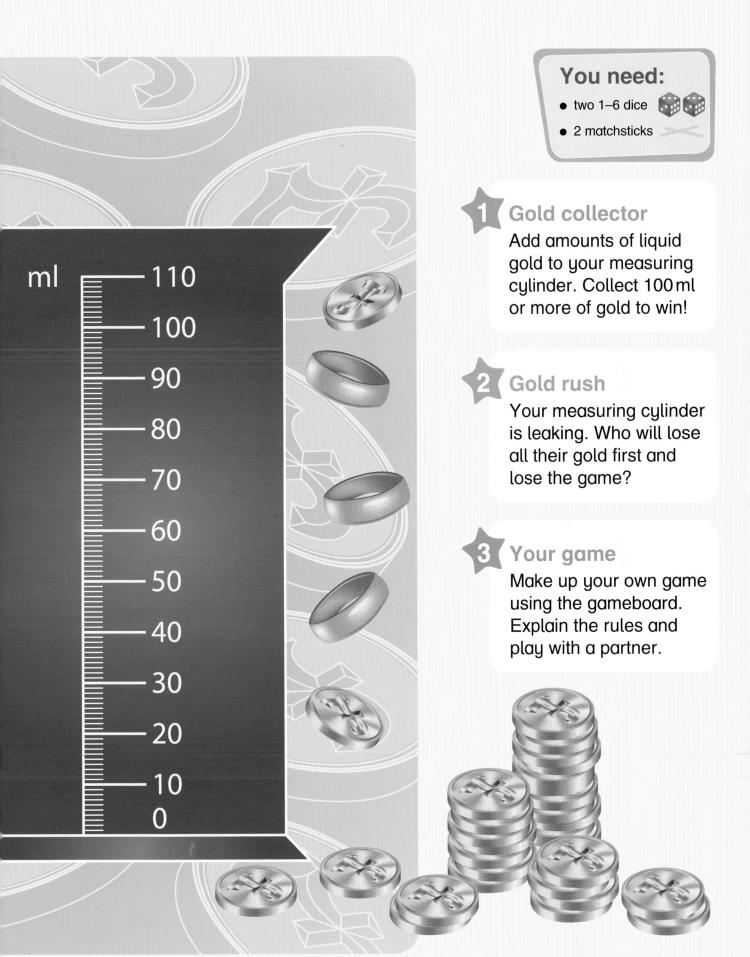

ml

110
100
90
80
70
60
50
40
30
20
10
0

1 Gold collector

Add amounts of liquid gold to your measuring cylinder. Collect 100 ml or more of gold to win!

2 Gold rush

Your measuring cylinder is leaking. Who will lose all their gold first and lose the game?

3 Your game

Make up your own game using the gameboard. Explain the rules and play with a partner.

And finally ...

Let's review

1

Lili is ill. The doctor gave her a 120 ml bottle of medicine.

a Lili takes 5 ml of medicine 3 times a day for a week. How much medicine does she take altogether?

b Draw a measuring cylinder with the left over medicine in.

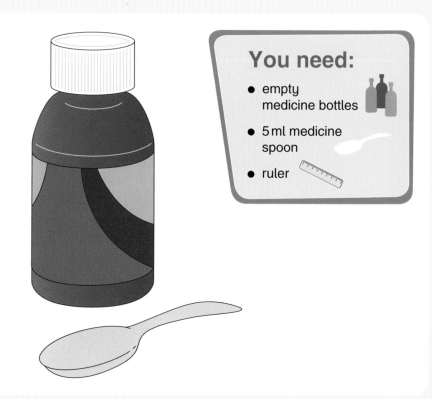

You need:

- empty medicine bottles
- 5 ml medicine spoon
- ruler

2

Copy and complete the table by finding $\frac{1}{3}$ of each amount.

You need:

- paper strips

Quantity	One third, $\frac{1}{3}$
1 minute	
60 ml of milk	
1 hour	
21 cm of string	
Bag of 27 sweets	
15p	
36 strawberries	
1 day	
3 pizzas	

Teacher's Guide

See pages 162–3 of the *Teacher's Guide* for guidance on running each task. Observe children to identify those who have mastered concepts and those who require further consolidation.

3

Seb is in Class 2M. He says they spend more time on English (including spelling, grammar and reading) than anything else. Is he right? How do you know?

2M Timetable

		9:00 – 10:10		10:30 – 11:25	11:30 – 12:00		1:15 – 2:15	2:15 – 3:15
Monday	9:00 – 9:15 Assembly	Mathematics	B	English	Reading	L	PE	PE
Tuesday	9:00 – 9:15 Assembly	Mathematics	R	English	Spelling & grammar	U	Topic	
Wednesday	9:00 – 9:15 Assembly	Mathematics	E	English	Reading	N	Topic	
Thursday	9:00 – 9:15 Assembly	Mathematics	A	English	Spelling & grammar	C	Topic	PE
Friday		Mathematics	K	English	Assembly	H	Topic	

Did you know?

Although recipes tell you exactly how much of a particular ingredient to use, chefs rarely use measuring equipment. They are so experienced that they know just what 100 g or 50 ml of something looks like, so they just estimate.

If you want your food to taste just as lovely as theirs, measure!

Solving problems

I wonder if that's enough paint to paint our classroom?

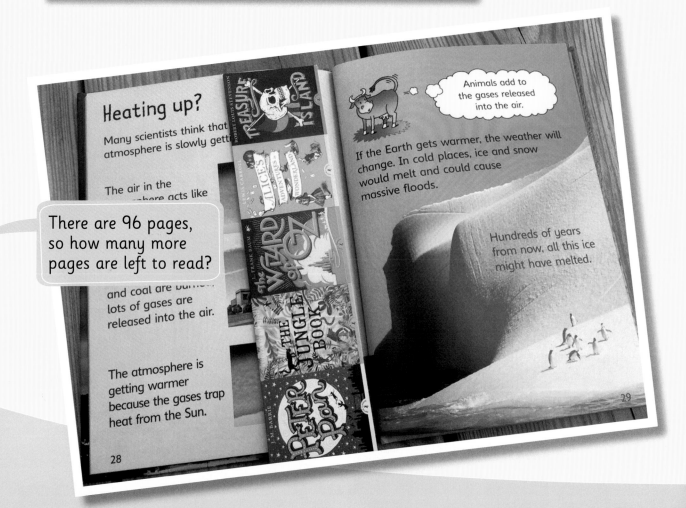

There are 96 pages, so how many more pages are left to read?

How many points do the guests need to score to catch up?

How much dog food is shown here?

2 kg
5 kg
10 kg
15 kg

I'll have the cone. What's my change from £1?

86p
74p

Teacher's Guide   Look at the pictures with the children and discuss the questions.
See pages 164–5 of the *Teacher's Guide* for key ideas to draw out.

151

Add or subtract?

Let's learn

You need:
- number rods
- Base 10 apparatus
- bead string
- counters or cubes

You can only use the bar model for problems with 2 parts and a whole.

No, you can have a whole and as many parts as you need!

Add or subtract?

Lili has 87 books. 29 are non-fiction and the rest are fiction. How many fiction books does she have?

Use the bar model to find out whether to add or subtract.

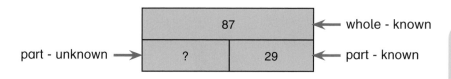

whole - known
part - unknown
part - known

part + part = whole, so whole − part = part

87 − 29 = 58 Lili has 58 fiction books.

You can use anything to help you work out the solution, e.g. a bead string or a number line.

More bars

If you know the parts but not the whole, add the parts:

part + part = whole.

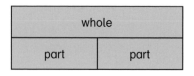

| whole | |
| part | part |

The 2 parts added together will be equal in value to the whole:

part + part = whole.

There might be 3 (or more) parts:

part + part + part = whole

whole − part − part = part.

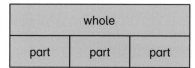

| whole | | |
| part | part | part |

If you know the whole but not the parts, there may be more than one solution!

Teacher's Guide

Before working through the *Textbook*, study page 166 of the *Teacher's Guide* to see how the concepts should be introduced. Read and discuss the page with the children. Provide concrete resources to support exploration.

Draw a set of bars to help solve each problem.

1 Answer these.

a   Seb is reading a book with 72 pages. He has read 53 pages. How many pages does he have left to read?

b   Yesterday, the temperature was 15 °C. It is 9 °C cooler today. What is the temperature today?

c   Lili scored 48 points on the first level of a computer game and 39 points on the second level. How many points did she score altogether?

d   Seb had 64 stickers. He then bought a pack of 15 stickers. How many stickers does he have now?

2 Answer this.

Seb drew these bars to help him work out how many girls were in his class today. If there are 3 more girls than boys, how many boys and girls are in Seb's class today?

27	
boys	girls

3 Solve.

Write 2 different problems for this set of bars. Decide what is unknown in each problem.

73	
16	57

Use metres in one problem and kilograms in the other.

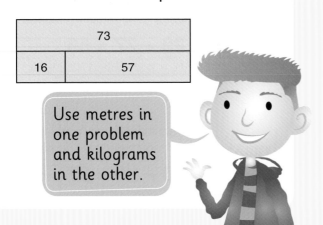

4 Think.

Lili, Seb and Oli have a different number of marbles each. They have 24 marbles altogether. They each have more than 6 but less than 10. How many marbles could each child have?

24		
Lili	Seb	Oli

Teacher's Guide

See page 167 of the *Teacher's Guide* for ideas of how to guide practice. Work through each step together as a class to develop children's conceptual understanding.

153 ★

Checking addition and subtraction

Let's learn

Checking addition is easy, you just add in a different order. You can't do that for subtraction, so you can't check it.

You can check it! You can add the difference onto the subtrahend to check.

Checking addition

To check an addition, add in a different order. You can also subtract the augend or addend from the total.

27 + 56 = 83
addend + augend = total

All the calculations are in the same fact family!

Add in a different order:

56 + 27 = 83
augend + addend = total

Subtract the addend or the augend from the total:

83 − 27 = 56
total − addend = augend

83 − 56 = 27
total − augend = addend

Checking subtraction

To check a subtraction, add the difference to the subtrahend. You can also subtract the difference from the minuend.

56 − 27 = 29
minuend − subtrahend = difference

Just rearranging the numbers may not show if you have made a mistake. You need to do the inverse calculation.

Add the difference and the subtrahend:

27 + 29 = 56
subtrahend + difference = minuend

29 + 27 = 56
difference + subtrahend = minuend

Subtract the difference from the minuend:

56 − 29 = 27
minuend − difference = subtrahend

Teacher's Guide

Before working through the *Textbook*, study page 168 of the *Teacher's Guide* to see how the concepts should be introduced. Read and discuss the page with the children. Provide concrete resources to support exploration.

1 Answer these.

Write a checking number statement for each calculation. Use apparatus to help you.

a   45 + 23 = 68
b   29 + 16 = 45
c   58 + 33 = 91

d   67 − 32 = 35
e   35 − 19 = 16
f   41 − 24 = 17

2 Answer these.

Which of these calculations have an answer between 60 and 70? Write the number statement and a checking number statement for each answer between 60 and 70.

a   36 + 36
b   95 − 27

c   46 + 17
d   98 − 32

e   29 + 32
f   85 − 31

3 Solve.

Write a number statement and a checking statement for each problem.

a   Seb needs 85 g of sugar to make biscuits, but there is only 18 g left in the packet. How much more sugar does he need?

b   Lili's dog is 38 cm tall. Seb's dog is 17 cm taller. How tall is Seb's dog?

4 Investigate.

I think of a number and subtract 17. I add 4 and the answer is 50. What was my number? How do you know?

Make up your own *I think of a number* and challenge a partner to tell you your number.

Teacher's Guide

See page 169 of the *Teacher's Guide* for ideas of how to guide practice. Work through each step together as a class to develop children's conceptual understanding.

155 ★

Solving missing number problems

You need:

- Base 10 apparatus or place-value counters
- number rods
- number line
- bead string

Let's learn

You have to find out how many more to add on to find a missing number, such as 13 add something equals 28.

It depends on the problem, sometimes it's easier to subtract. If I subtract 13 from 28, I know that the missing number is 15.

Addition

You can use what you know about checking calculations to find missing numbers:

Subtract the augend from the total:

48 + ▢ = 72 ⟶ **72 − 48 = 24**

augend + addend = total · · · · · · total − augend = addend

Subtract the addend from the total:

▢ + 24 = 72 ⟶ **72 − 24 = 48**

augend + addend = total · · · · · · total − addend = augend

You're just undoing the addition!

Subtraction

Subtract the difference from the minuend:

72 − ▢ = 48 ⟶ **72 − 48 = 24**

minuend - subtrahend = difference · · · · · · minuend − difference = subtrahend

You're just doing what you did to check a subtraction!

Add the difference to the subtrahend:

▢ − 24 = 48 ⟶ **48 + 24 = 72**

minuend − subtrahend = difference · · · · · · difference + subtrahend = minuend

You're just undoing the subtraction!

Teacher's Guide

Before working through the *Textbook*, study page 170 of the *Teacher's Guide* to see how the concepts should be introduced. Read and discuss the page with the children. Provide concrete resources to support exploration.

★ **156**

1 Answer these.

Find the missing number. Write the number statement that you used.

a $25 + \boxed{} = 38$

b $\boxed{} + 36 = 84$

c $64 - \boxed{} = 21$

d $\boxed{} - 56 = 35$

2 Answer these.

Write the 8 number statements in the fact family shown by this set of bars. Use an empty box to show the unknown number. One has been done for you.

65	
27	?

$27 + \boxed{} = 65$

What is the missing number?

3 Apply.

Write a missing number statement for each problem and the number statement you used to find the missing number.

Draw a set of bars to help you.

a   Maya is helping to lay a path in the garden. In the morning they laid 24 metres of path. By 5 o'clock, they had finished the 56-metre-long path. What length of path did they lay in the afternoon?

b   Thomas and Rosie went strawberry picking. They picked 28 kg of strawberries altogether. Thomas picked 13 kg.
How many kilograms did Rosie pick?

4 Think.

Which single digits could go in the boxes to make this calculation correct?

$6\boxed{} - 3\boxed{} = 31$

Find all the possible answers.

How do you know you have found them all?

Teacher's Guide

See page 171 of the *Teacher's Guide* for ideas of how to guide practice. Work through each step together as a class to develop children's conceptual understanding.

157

You need:
- place-value cards
- Base 10 apparatus

Let's learn

You always write a calculation in a line, so 32 + 25 = 57.

You can also write in columns! It shows the place value of each digit.

Adding in columns

Writing addition in columns shows the place value of the numbers.

32 + 26

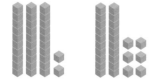

```
  32
+ 26
────
  50   add the tens
   8   add the ones
────
  58   add the tens and ones
```

It's just partitioning to add!

38 + 47

```
  38
+ 47
────
  70   add the tens
  15   add the ones
────
  85   add the tens and ones
```

Teacher's Guide

Before working through the *Textbook*, study page 172 of the *Teacher's Guide* to see how the concepts should be introduced. Read and discuss the page with the children. Provide concrete resources to support exploration.

1 **Answer these.**

Use column addition to solve each number statement.

a 24 + 45
b 37 + 56
c 69 + 18
d 32 + 29

Remember, it's just like partitioning!

2 **Answer these.**

Find the missing digit, or digits, in each calculation. Write the complete calculations.

a
```
  47
+ 2▮
────
  60
  11
────
  71
```

b
```
  52
+ ▮5
────
  80
   7
────
  87
```

c
```
  3▮
+ ▮8
────
  50
   9
────
  59
```

d
```
  ▮6
+ 1▮
────
  40
  15
────
  55
```

3 **Apply.**

Add in columns to find the total amounts.

a Noah's dad bought a 28 kg sack of potatoes and a 24 kg sack of carrots. How heavy was his shopping?

b Hafsa's mum spent £38 on fruit and £17 on vegetables. How much did she spend?

c Seb bought a pair of jeans for £26 and a pair of trainers for £45. How much did he spend?

d Lili bought 2 pieces of wood to make shelves. The first piece was 43 cm long, the second was 49 cm long. How many centimetres of wood did she buy?

4 **Think.**

Find 5 pairs of 2-digit numbers where:

The total of the 2 numbers is 73.

Can you find a pair where the difference between the numbers is 17?

Record your additions in columns. Choose how to record your subtractions.

Teacher's Guide
See page 173 of the *Teacher's Guide* for ideas of how to guide practice. Work through each step together as a class to develop children's conceptual understanding.

159 ★

Checkpoint!

Let's play

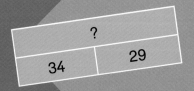

	?	
34		29

	76	
27		?

Start

34 + 29

94 – 49

35 + 57　64 – 29　30 – 17

94 – 45

53 + 31

76 – 27

45 + 49　　85 – 23

70 – 46

46 + 24

17 + 13　　79 – 38

51 – 15

36 + 15

24 + 46

92 – 57

49 + 45

23 + 62　30 – 13　27 + 49　92 – 35　15 + 36

Teacher's Guide

See pages 174–5 of the *Teacher's Guide*. Explain the rules for each game and allow children to choose which to play. Encourage them to challenge themselves and practise what they have learnt in the unit.

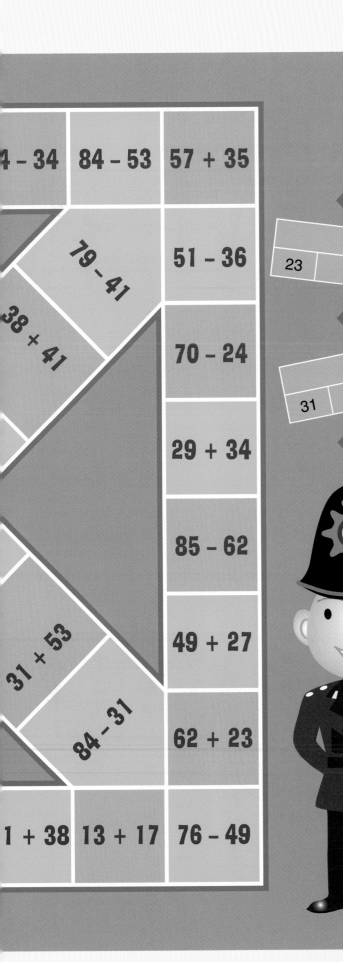

4 – 34 | 84 – 53 | 57 + 35

79 – 41

38 + 41

51 – 36

70 – 24

29 + 34

85 – 62

31 + 53

84 – 31

49 + 27

62 + 23

1 + 38 | 13 + 17 | 76 – 49

	?	
23		62

	84	
31		?

1 Check it!

Collect 6 calculations and a checking statement for each one. First player back to Start is the winner.

2 Family check

Collect 3 calculations and the 3 checking calculations from the same fact family for each one. First player back to Start is the winner.

3 Your game

Design your own game. Explain the rules and play with a partner.

12 And finally ...

1 Copy and complete each set of bars.
What do you notice?

You need:
- number rods

35	
17	18

?	
27	28

?	
7	8

95	
47	?

Draw and label 2 more sets of bars which could
be part of the same group of bars.

Write a problem which could be solved using 1
of these sets of bars.

2 What subtractions can you use to check
these additions?

You need:
- Base 10 apparatus

46 g + 29 g	39 m + 38 m
38 cm + 26 cm	52 kg + 29 kg
45 g + 27 g	43 m + 19 m

What additions can you use to check these subtractions?

37 g – 19 g	71 m – 38 m
45 cm – 26 cm	52 kg – 35 kg
85 g – 47 g	63 m – 34 m

Teacher's Guide

See pages 176–7 of the *Teacher's Guide* for guidance on running each task.
Observe children to identify those who have mastered concepts and those who
require further consolidation.

3 Copy this crossnumber puzzle onto squared paper. Colour in the dark squares so that you do not write any numbers in those squares. Solve the clues to complete the puzzle. Write each digit of your answer in a new square.

Across

1. 34
    + 38

2. 27
    + 27

3. 55
    + 34

4. $21 + \blacksquare = 99$

5. $\blacksquare - 25 = 36$

7. $\blacksquare - 42 = 55$

8. $\blacksquare + 23 = 89$

9. $18 + \blacksquare = 81$

10. $91 = \blacksquare = 32$

Down

1. 43
    + 36

2. 32
    + 26

3. 59
    + 27

4. 46
    + 25

5. $99 - \blacksquare = 32$

6. $100 - \blacksquare = 54$

7. 39
    + 54

8. $\blacksquare - 45 = 24$

Did you know?

The first person to use a symbol to represent an unknown number is believed to be Diophantus of Alexandria, Ancient Greece, around the year AD 245. He used a symbol a bit like this: ς. Diophantus was one of the first people to write problems using symbols instead of words.

Seven added to five equals twelve became 7 + 5 = 12.

Counting in threes, fractions and time

How many?

How much has been eaten?

5 METALLIC MARKERS £4.99

5 METALLIC MARKERS

5 METALLIC MARKERS

How many pens are there?

I wonder what the time is?

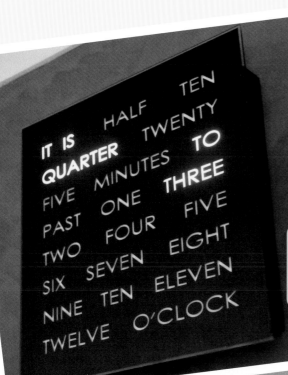

IT IS HALF TEN
QUARTER TWENTY TO
FIVE MINUTES PAST ONE THREE
TWO FOUR FIVE
SIX SEVEN EIGHT
NINE TEN ELEVEN
TWELVE O'CLOCK

I wonder how you tell the time using this clock?

Teacher's Guide

Look at the pictures with the children and discuss the questions.
See pages 178–9 of the *Teacher's Guide* for key ideas to draw out.

165

Multiplication table for 3

Let's learn

3 is an odd number, so all the products in the multiplication table for 3 must be odd.

That's not right! 3, 6, 9, 12, 15, 18 ... The products are odd, even, odd, even, odd, even ...

Counting in threes

0 1 2 3 4 5 6 7 8 9 10 11 12 13 14 15 16 17 18 19 20 21 22 23 24 25 26 27 28 29 30 31 32 33 34 35 36

Count in threes. Start from 0 and keep on adding 3.

Which numbers are on the last 4 cards?

| 3 | 6 | 9 | 12 | 15 | 18 | 21 | 24 | | | | |

Multiplication table for 3

Build the multiplication table for 3 with sets of tricycle wheels.

3 × 1 = 3

3 × 2 = 6

3 × 3 = 9

3 × 4 = 12

3 × 5 = 15

3 × 6 = 18

The product of 3 × 5 is the same in the multiplication table for 5: 5 × 3 = 15.
I know that 15 ÷ 5 = 3 and 15 ÷ 3 = 5 too!

If you carry on to 12 tricycles, you will have written the multiplication table for 3!

1 Answer these.

Copy and complete these sequences.

a   3, 6, 9, ▢ , ▢

c   18, 21, 24, ▢ , ▢

b   36, 33, 30, ▢ , ▢

d   21, 18, 15, ▢ , ▢

2 Write.

This array shows that 3 × 10 = 30 and 30 = 10 × 3.
Write the 3 other pairs of multiplication and division
statements shown by the array.

3 Apply.

Kia the kangaroo makes
jumps of 3 m along the path.

How far does she travel with:

a   3 jumps?

b   6 jumps?

c   9 jumps?

How many jumps does she need
to travel:

d   12 m?

e   21 m?

f   36 m?

Write the matching multiplication
statements.

4 Investigate.

Calculate a digit sum
by adding together the
digits of a number.

12: 1 + 2 = 3. The digit
sum of 12 is 3.

Investigate the digit
sums of the products in
the multiplication table
for 3 up to 36.

What do
you notice?

Teacher's Guide

See page 181 of the *Teacher's Guide* for ideas of how to guide practice.
Work through each step together as a class to develop children's
conceptual understanding.

167 ★

You need:

- paper strips
- 30 cm ruler
- interlocking cubes
- string
- balance scales
- 1 kg weights

Let's learn

4 is greater than 3, so $\frac{1}{4}$ is greater than $\frac{1}{3}$.

No. Quarters divide a quantity into 4 equal parts. Thirds divide a quantity into 3 equal parts, so $\frac{1}{3}$ is greater than $\frac{1}{4}$.

Fraction number lines

Fractions are numbers too.

| 0 | | $\frac{1}{2}$ | | 1 | | $1\frac{1}{2}$ | | 2 | | $2\frac{1}{2}$ | | 3 | | $3\frac{1}{2}$ | | 4 |

| 0 | $\frac{1}{3}$ | $\frac{2}{3}$ | 1 | $1\frac{1}{3}$ | $1\frac{2}{3}$ | 2 | $2\frac{1}{3}$ | $2\frac{2}{3}$ | 3 | $3\frac{1}{3}$ | $3\frac{2}{3}$ | 4 |

| 0 | $\frac{1}{4}$ | $\frac{2}{4}$ | $\frac{3}{4}$ | 1 | $1\frac{1}{4}$ | $1\frac{2}{4}$ | $1\frac{3}{4}$ | 2 | $2\frac{1}{4}$ | $2\frac{2}{4}$ | $2\frac{3}{4}$ | 3 | $3\frac{1}{4}$ | $3\frac{2}{4}$ | $3\frac{3}{4}$ | 4 |

I can see that $\frac{1}{3}$ is greater than $\frac{1}{4}$, because $\frac{1}{3}$ is further along the number line.

And $\frac{2}{4}$ is the same as $\frac{1}{2}$. Look, $\frac{1}{2}$ is in the same place as $\frac{2}{4}$, so is $1\frac{1}{2}$ and $1\frac{2}{4}$, $2\frac{1}{2}$ and $2\frac{2}{4}$, and $3\frac{1}{2}$ and $3\frac{2}{4}$!

Scaling up and down

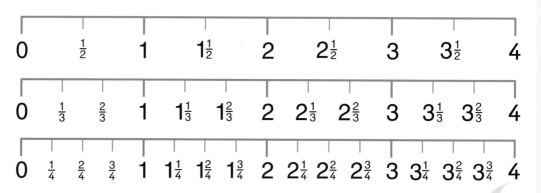

Twice as big

3 × as big

$\frac{1}{2}$ the size

$\frac{1}{3}$ the size

If each small blue part is 5, the larger part must be 10, because 5 × 2 = 10.

If each large yellow part is 30, the smaller part must be 10, because 30 ÷ 3 = 10, $\frac{1}{3}$ of 30 = 10.

What is twice the length of a 30 cm ruler?

What is $\frac{1}{3}$ of a 60 cm piece of wood?

Teacher's Guide

Before working through the *Textbook*, study page 182 of the *Teacher's Guide* to see how the concepts should be introduced. Read and discuss the page with the children. Provide concrete resources to support exploration.

1 Answer this.

Which numbers are missing from each number line?

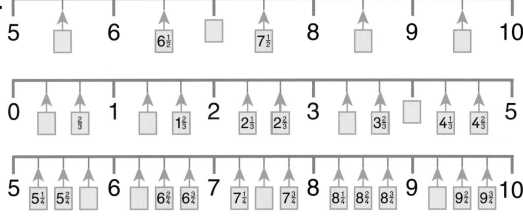

---

2 Copy and complete.

$\frac{1}{3}$ the size	$\frac{1}{2}$ the size	Size	Twice as big	3 times as big
		6		
		12		
		24		
		36		

---

3 Apply.

a Lilli's dog is 90 cm tall. Seb's dog is half as tall and Molly's dog is $\frac{1}{3}$ as tall. How tall are they?

b Seb's toy snake is 15 cm long. At the shop, 1 toy snake is twice as long and another 3 times as long. How long are they?

c A bag of rice weighs 2 kg. Small bags weigh half as much and large bags weigh twice as much. Special offer bags weigh 3 times as much. How heavy is each bag?

4 Think.

Make a creature using interlocking cubes. Now make another one twice as big.
Can you make one half the size or another 3 times as big?

Teacher's Guide
See page 183 of the *Teacher's Guide* for ideas of how to guide practice. Work through each step together as a class to develop children's conceptual understanding.

169 ⭐

You need:
- analogue clock
- printed blank clock faces
- 24-hour timeline
- counters
- paper strips

Let's learn

It takes 3 hours to get to Grandma's.

No. Our train goes at 25 minutes past 3 and arrives at 25 minutes to 6. You can't ignore the minutes. It's only 2 hours and 10 minutes.

24 hours in a day

The Earth spins once every 24 hours. This is 1 whole day.

What time do you wake up?
What time do you go to bed?

Day

Night

Sun

12 o'clock midnight | 1 o'clock | 2 o'clock | 3 o'clock | 4 o'clock | 5 o'clock | 6 o'clock | 7 o'clock | 8 o'clock | 9 o'clock | 10 o'clock | 11 o'clock | 12 o'clock midday | 1 o'clock | 2 o'clock | 3 o'clock | 4 o'clock | 5 o'clock | 6 o'clock | 7 o'clock | 8 o'clock | 9 o'clock | 10 o'clock | 11 o'clock | 12 o'clock midnight

How long?

To find out how long something takes, you need to know the start and end times.

train leaves 25 past 3   train arrives 25 to 6

Count the hours:

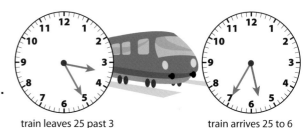

1 hour to   2 hours to

Calculate the minutes:
25 minutes past 5 to 25 minutes to 6 = 10 minutes

25 past 3   25 past 4   25 past 5

25 to 6

1 hour   1 hour   10 minutes

2 o'clock   3 o'clock   4 o'clock   5 o'clock   6 o'clock   7 o'clock

Total time = 2 hours and 10 minutes.

Teacher's Guide

Before working through the *Textbook*, study page 184 of the *Teacher's Guide* to see how the concepts should be introduced. Read and discuss the page with the children. Provide concrete resources to support exploration.

1 Answer these.

How many hours in:

a $\frac{3}{4}$ of a day?

b $\frac{1}{2}$ of a day?

c $\frac{1}{3}$ of a day?

d $2\frac{3}{4}$ days?

e $\frac{1}{4}$ of a day?

f $1\frac{1}{2}$ days?

> Remember there are 24 hours in 1 day.

2 Answer.

On Time TV, the programmes are all the same length on a particular day.

Copy and complete the table.

Day	Programme length	Number of programmes
Monday	2 hours	
Tuesday	$\frac{1}{2}$ hour	
Wednesday	4 hours	
Thursday	$\frac{1}{3}$ hour	
Friday	$\frac{3}{4}$ hour	
Saturday	3 hours	
Sunday	1 hour	

3 Apply.

Copy and complete the table. How long does each journey take?

Put the journeys in order from shortest to longest.

Journey	Start	End	Journey time
A	Quarter to 4	25 minutes to 9	
B	10 minutes past 10	10 minutes to 3	
C	Half past 8	Quarter past 1	
D	5 minutes past 11	20 minutes to 4	

4 Investigate.

Choose 4 times when the hands on a clock make (or very nearly make) a straight line, e.g. 5 minutes past 7.

Order your times from earliest to latest.

Find the interval between each time.

What was your shortest and longest time interval?

> What was your shortest and longest time interval?

Teacher's Guide

See page 185 of the *Teacher's Guide* for ideas of how to guide practice. Work through each step together as a class to develop children's conceptual understanding.

171 ⭐

Threes

6	18	3	27	30
27	30	12	3	21
36	9	15	24	33
15	6	9	3	12
21	24	30	18	9

Teacher's Guide

See pages 186–7 of the *Teacher's Guide*. Explain the rules for each game and allow children to choose which to play. Encourage them to challenge themselves and practise what they have learnt in the unit.

 1 4 in a row

Spin the spinner. Multiply by 3 and cover the product on the grid. Be the first to make a row of 4 to win!

 2 Dividing by 3

Choose a dividend to divide by 3. Cover as many squares as you can by making correct division statements!

 3 Your game

Make up your own game using the gameboard.

And finally ...

Let's review

1

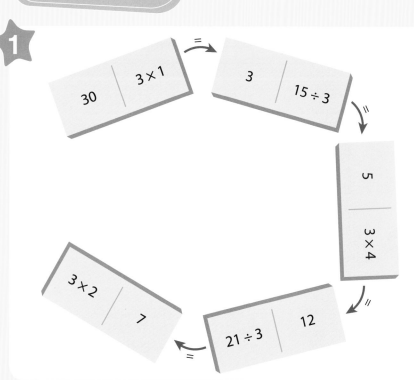

You need:

- 24 blank dominoes
- stopwatch

Use all your multiplication and division facts for 3 to make a set of 24 dominoes.

How quickly can you arrange them in a loop?

2

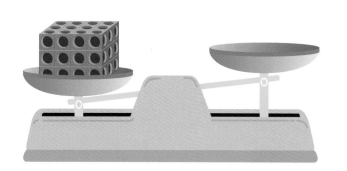

You need:

- interlocking cubes
- cuboid made of interlocking cubes
- balance scales
- small objects

I wonder what objects have half the mass of the cuboid?

What about a quarter, a third or 3 quarters of the cuboid? Or a cuboid twice as heavy or 3 times as heavy as this one?

Make fractions or multiples of the cuboid that can be used to weigh objects in your classroom.

Teacher's Guide

See pages 188–9 of the *Teacher's Guide* for guidance on running each task. Observe children to identify those who have mastered concepts and those who require further consolidation.

3

Make a timeline with 24 squares showing each hour from 12 o'clock midnight to 12 o'clock midnight.

Use a key to colour the squares, showing what you do in that hour.

Do this for a school day and a non-school day.

How are the 2 days the same?
How are they different?

Compare your days with someone else.
How are they the same?
How are they different?

You need:

- 2 strips of large squared paper, 24 squares long
- coloured pencils

Key
- ■ school
- ■ asleep
- ■ playing
- □ computer
- ▨ watch TV

Did you know?

Some old clocks were made with a 24-hour face. This means the hour hand goes just once around the clock face in a day. This clock is on the wall of the old town hall in Prague, Czech Republic. It was made in 1410 so is more than 600 years old.

Notice how it only has an hour hand.

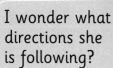

I wonder what directions she is following?

I wonder what this road sign means.

How can you open this bottle?

I wonder how long this baby turtle is.

Which one is the furthest away?

Teacher's Guide

Look at the pictures with the children and discuss the questions.
See pages 190–1 of the *Teacher's Guide* for key ideas to draw out.

177 ★

You need:
- geostrips
- 1–6 dice
- clock with moveable hands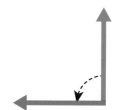

Let's learn

A quarter turn is called a right angle. I think both of these angles are right angles.

Only the first one is a right angle. The second one shows more than a quarter turn.

Quarter turns and right angles

These quarter turns are right angles.

Clockwise and anticlockwise turns

A turn moving the same way as the clock's hands is clockwise.

A turn moving the opposite way to the clock's hands is anticlockwise.

Clockwise:

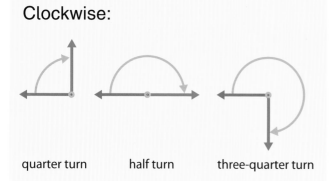

quarter turn   half turn   three-quarter turn

Anticlockwise:

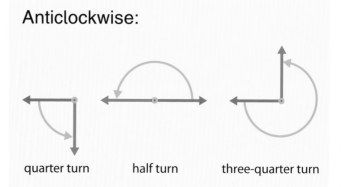

quarter turn   half turn   three-quarter turn

Teacher's Guide

Before working through the *Textbook*, study page 192 of the *Teacher's Guide* to see how the concepts should be introduced. Read and discuss the page with the children. Provide concrete resources to support exploration.

1 Find.

Identify the turns that make right angles.

Are they clockwise or anticlockwise?

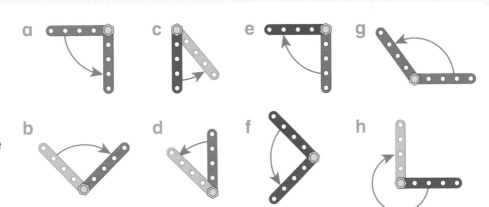

2 Find.

The hour hand makes these turns. What number does it stop on?

 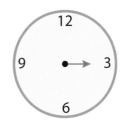

a quarter turn clockwise

b three-quarter turn anticlockwise

c half a turn clockwise

d half a turn anticlockwise

3 Apply.

Roll a dice and turn that many quarter turns clockwise from 12 o'clock. The winner is the player with the later time after each roll. What is the latest time you could make with 4 rolls?

What is the smallest number of rolls to get to 12 o'clock again?

4 Think.

The purple shape is turned to make each pattern. Describe the size and direction of each turn.

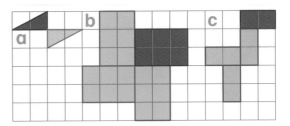

Can you think of a different way?

Teacher's Guide
See page 193 of the *Teacher's Guide* for ideas of how to guide practice. Work through each step together as a class to develop children's conceptual understanding.

179 ★

Estimating lengths and distances

You need:

- 30 cm ruler
- metre stick

Let's learn

I think our classroom must be about 100 metres long.

That's not right! A football pitch is about 100 metres long. Our classroom isn't as big as that! It may be nearer to 10 metres long.

Estimating length

Estimating is making a sensible guess based on what you know.

Measuring length tells you how long something is.

To estimate a length, you could compare it to a ruler or metre stick.

 The sides of this square are about 2 cm long.

Estimating distance

Distance measures the space between 2 points.

You estimate distance to find:

- how far something has travelled
- how long a journey will be.

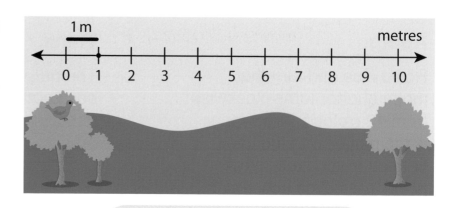

If the bird is about 1 m away from the small tree, it is about 10 m away from the big tree.

Teacher's Guide

Before working through the *Textbook*, study page 194 of the *Teacher's Guide* to see how the concepts should be introduced. Read and discuss the page with the children. Provide concrete resources to support exploration.

1 Estimate.

Estimate the length of each line. Record your estimates.

Measure the length of each line.

Compare with your estimates.

a ▬▬▬▬

b ▬▬▬▬▬▬▬▬▬

c ▬▬▬▬▬▬▬▬▬▬▬▬▬▬▬

d ▬▬▬▬▬▬▬▬▬▬▬▬▬

2 Copy and complete.

Estimate these lengths.

Now measure using a ruler or a metre stick

	Estimate	Measure
Length of your classroom		
Length of your desk		
Length of your pencil case		

3 Measure.

Go to the hall or corridor.

Walk forwards until you think you have walked:

a   1 metre

b   2 metres

c   4 metres

Mark each distance.

Measure how far you have walked.

4 Investigate.

Find an object in the classroom which you think is:

a   about 30 cm long

b   about $\frac{1}{2}$ m

c   about 1 m

d   shorter than 1 m

Copy the number line. Draw a picture of each object by the number line to show its size.

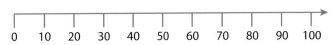

Teacher's Guide

See page 195 of the *Teacher's Guide* for ideas of how to guide practice.
Work through each step together as a class to develop children's
conceptual understanding.

181 ✦

You need:
- squared paper
- card robot
- clock

Let's learn

To get the car to the garage, I would say: 'Go forward, turn clockwise'.

You need to give clearer directions! 'Go forward 3 squares. Make 1 right-angle turn clockwise, go forward 3 squares'.

Following directions

To follow directions:
- face in the correct direction
- listen carefully.

Follow the robot's path:
- go forward 2 squares.
- make $\frac{1}{4}$ turn anticlockwise.
- go forward 2 squares.

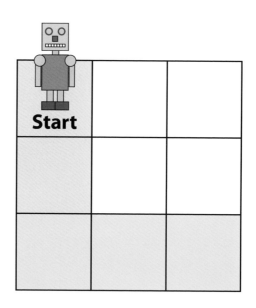

Start

Writing directions

Use this checklist to help you write clear directions:

1 Work out where to start and finish. ✔
2 Include which direction to face. ✔
3 Include number of steps/squares to move. ✔
4 Describe any turns carefully. ✔

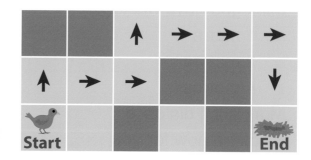

Can you write directions for the bird to reach the nest?

Teacher's Guide

Before working through the *Textbook*, study page 196 of the *Teacher's Guide* to see how the concepts should be introduced. Read and discuss the page with the children. Provide concrete resources to support exploration.

1 Follow directions.

Will these directions take the yellow ship to the gold?

Go forward 4 squares.
Make 1 right-angle turn clockwise.
Go forward 1 square.
Make 1 right-angle turn anticlockwise.
Go forward 2 squares.
Make 1 right-angle turn anticlockwise.
Go forward 3 squares.

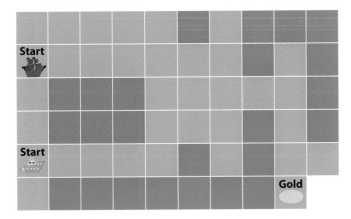

2 Copy and complete.

Copy and complete the directions for the pirate ship to get the gold.

Pirate ship
Go forward ____ squares
Make 1 right-angle turn clockwise
Go _____
Make _____
Go _____
Make _____
Go _____

3 Plan.

A postman is collecting letters from 2 post offices.

Write clear instructions so he avoids:
- closed roads
- a traffic jam
- a river.

Act this out in the playground. Use steps to measure the distance.

4 Think.

Copy the grid below.
Write instructions to teach a robot to travel in the shape of:

a   a small square
b   a large square

Start			

Teacher's Guide
See page 197 of the *Teacher's Guide* for ideas of how to guide practice. Work through each step together as a class to develop children's conceptual understanding.

183

Turn and jump!

Let's play

Start	1	2	3	4	5	6
9	10	11	12	13	14	15
18	19	20	21	22	23	24
27	28	29	30	31	32	33
36	37	38	39	40	41	42
45	46	47	48	49	50	51

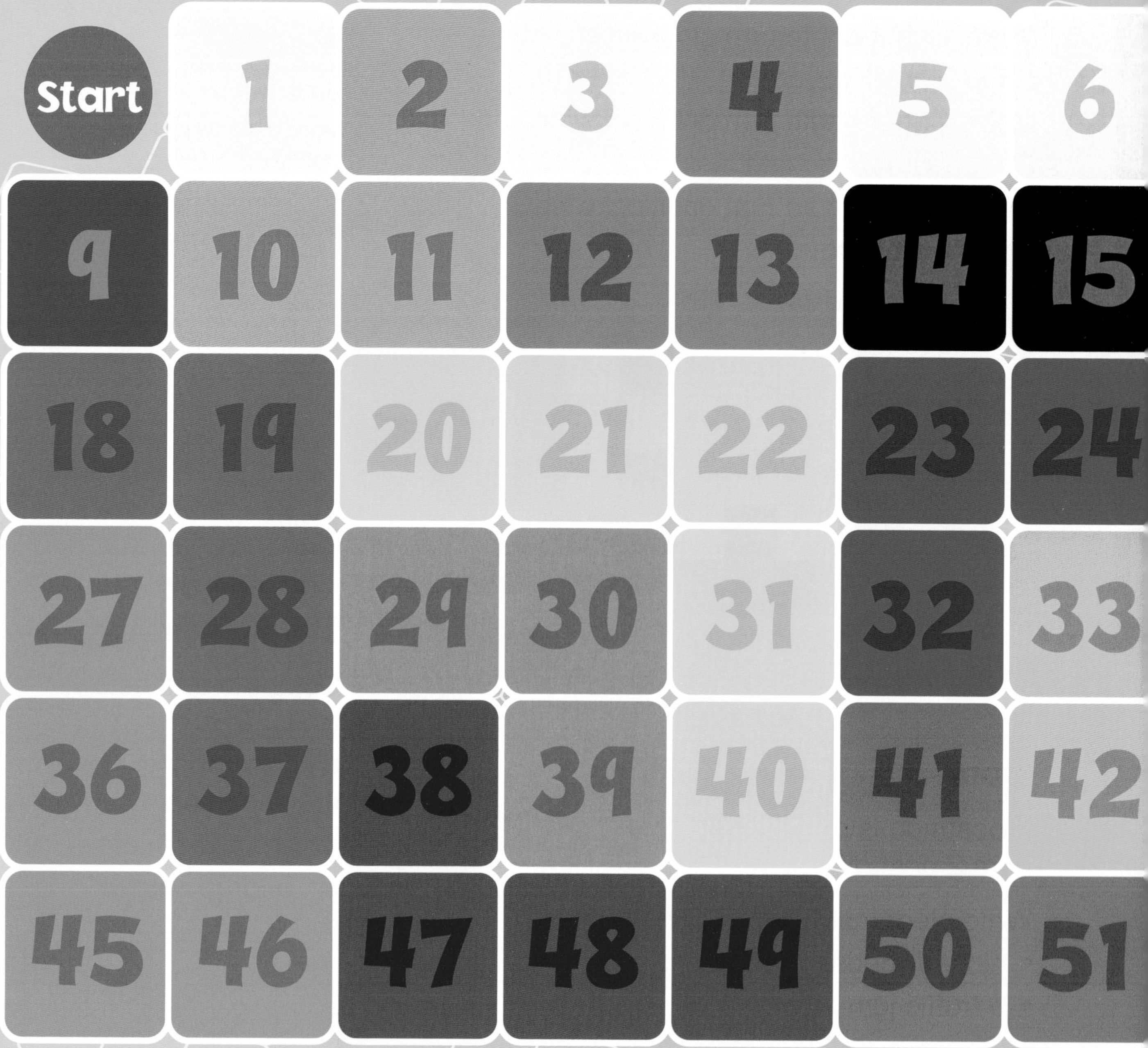

Teacher's Guide

See pages 198–9 of the *Teacher's Guide*. Explain the rules for each game and allow children to choose which to play. Encourage them to challenge themselves and practise what they have learnt in the unit.

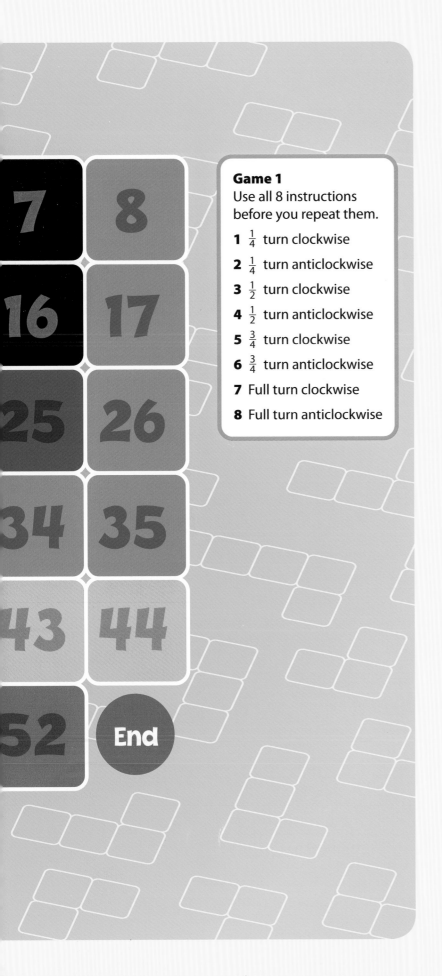

Game 1
Use all 8 instructions before you repeat them.

1 $\frac{1}{4}$ turn clockwise

2 $\frac{1}{4}$ turn anticlockwise

3 $\frac{1}{2}$ turn clockwise

4 $\frac{1}{2}$ turn anticlockwise

5 $\frac{3}{4}$ turn clockwise

6 $\frac{3}{4}$ turn anticlockwise

7 Full turn clockwise

8 Full turn anticlockwise

1 Turn

Turn at a right-angle to collect points. Who will collect the most?

2 Jump

Jump along shapes of the same colour to collect points. Who will win?

3 Your game

Make up your own game using the gameboard. Explain the rules and play with a partner.

Let's review

1

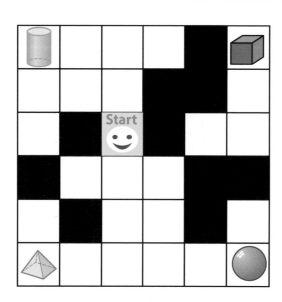

You need:

- 3-D shapes
- squared paper
- programmable toy

Give clear instructions from Start to collect 3 of the shapes.

Move forwards only. Turn clockwise and anticlockwise.

The black obstacles stop you collecting 1 shape. Which shape is it?

2

The orange shape is turned to make shapes A, B and C. Describe how the orange shape is moved to:

a shape A

b shape B

c shape C

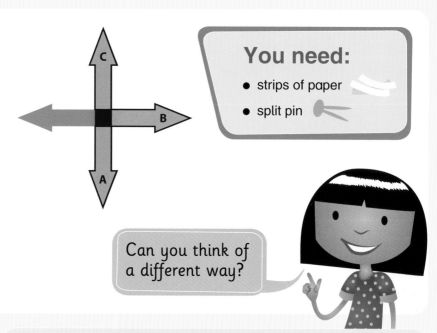

You need:

- strips of paper
- split pin

Can you think of a different way?

Teacher's Guide
See pages 200–1 of the *Teacher's Guide* for guidance on running each task. Observe children to identify those who have mastered concepts and those who require further consolidation.

3

Estimate how far the cars will travel.

Draw a line to show where you think they will stop.

Roll the cars down the ramp.

Did the cars travel further or less than you estimated?

You need:
- cardboard
- chair
- toy cars
- metre stick

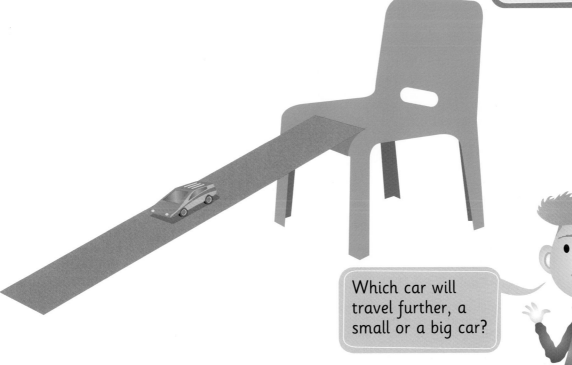

Which car will travel further, a small or a big car?

Did you know?

An aeroplane can't just fly anywhere. It follows directions from the control centre in the airport. There are paths in the sky that aeroplanes follow.

Invisible roads! The computers at the airport show the paths that the planes need to follow.

2 Glossary

2-dimensional (2-D)

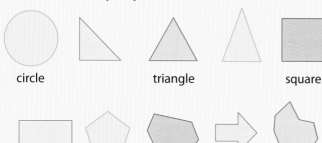

circle   triangle   square

rectangle   pentagon   hexagon   heptagon   octagon

3-dimensional (3-D)

cube   cuboid   cone   cylinder

sphere   triangular prism   triangular-based pyramid (tetrahedron)   square-based pyramid

5, 10, 15 … minutes past

Ways of counting minutes on an analogue clock. The minute hand takes five minutes to move between each hour mark on the clock face. See also *analogue clock*.

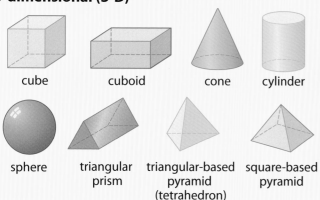

A

addend

The number being added in an addition calculation.

addition

A mathematical operation combining 2 or more numbers to find a total. Augend + addend = sum (or total).

$$3 + 5 = 8$$

augend   addend   sum/total

analogue clock

A dial with hands used to show time. The dial shows 12 hours in a full circle. The minute hand moves 1 complete turn every hour.

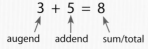
minute hand, hour hand

array

An arrangement of numbers, shapes or objects in rows of equal size and columns of equal size, used to find out how many altogether.

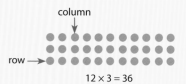
column, row $12 \times 3 = 36$

augend

The number being added to in an addition calculation. augend + addend = sum (or total)

$$3 + 5 = 8$$

augend   addend   sum/total

B

balance

Things are balanced when both sides have equal value, e.g. 3 + 4 = 2 and 100 g = 1 kg.

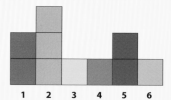

block diagram

A diagram showing information. Each block stands for one object or event.

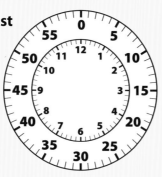

1 2 3 4 5 6

C

calendar

A list of the days of the year, arranged by month, week and day.

capacity

The amount a container holds. It is measured in litres or millilitres, e.g. the capacity of a 2-litre bottle is 2 litres.

Carroll diagram

A Carroll diagram sorts objects according to a criteria and not that criteria. There can be 2 different criteria, but always the criteria and not the criteria ,

	odd	not odd
< 50	23	18
not < 50	57	92

e.g. odd numbers/not odd numbers, multiples of 5/not multiples of 5, dogs/not dogs.

category

A group of elements or numbers all with the same property, e.g. dogs , cats, rats are all in the category 'animals'.

centimetre

A unit of length, 1 metre = 100 centimetres. Symbol: cm.

change

The money left over when buying something with a note or coin bigger than the amount needed. The change is given back to the buyer.

circular

Like a circle.

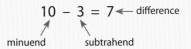

clockwise, anticlockwise

Clockwise: turning in the same direction as the hands on a clock. Anticlockwise: turning in the opposite direction to the hands on a clock.

column

A list of numbers, shapes or objects down a page, not across, often in a table or an array.

commutative

Addition and multiplication are commutative. It does not matter which way you add or multiply in, the answer is always the same. Same answer, different calculation, e.g. 3 + 4 = 4 + 3. But subtraction and division are not commutative, e.g. 7 − 2 ≠ 2 − 7.

cone

A 3-D shape with a flat, circular face and a curved face. It has one apex (sometimes mistakenly called a vertex) directly above the circular base.

cube

A 3-D shape made from six identical squares which all meet at right angles, e.g. a cube of sugar.

cuboid

A 3-D shape made from 6 rectangles. 2 or 4 of the rectangles could be squares, e.g. a cereal box. A cube is a special sort of cuboid.

curved, curved surface

A surface of a 3-D shape which is not flat, e.g. the surface of a sphere or the side of a cylinder.

cylinder

A 3-D shape with circular ends and one curved face joining the 2 circular faces.

D

degree

A unit of temperature. °C for degrees Celsius, though Centigrade is often still used.

denominator

The number underneath the line in a fraction. Also called the divisor.

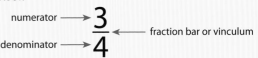

difference

The result of a subtraction, e.g. the difference between 12 and 5 is 7. See also *minuend*, *subtrahend*.

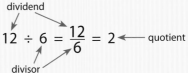

digit

The symbols 0, 1, 2, 3, 4, 5, 6, 7, 8 and 9. The value of each digit depends on its position, e.g. in 16, the digit 1 represents one ten while the 6 represents six ones.

dividend

The number that is divided in a division calculation, e.g. in 12 ÷ 6 = 2, 12 is the dividend. See also *denominator*, *divisor*, *quotient*.

division

A mathematical operation which shares or groups a quantity into a given number of parts, e.g. 12 ÷ 4 is 12 divided into 4 parts, each of value 3. It is the inverse operation to multiplication.

divisor

The number that is used to divide in a division sum, e.g. in 12 ÷ 6 = 2, 6 is the divisor. See also *denominator*, *dividend*, *quotient*.

double

Two lots of something, multiply by 2.

E

edge

The line made where 2 faces of a 3-D shape meet. See also *face*, *vertex*.

equals, equivalent

Symbol: =. Means to have the same value as, e.g. 5 + 3 = 7 + 1.

equivalent fractions

Fractions with the same value, e.g. $\frac{2}{4} = \frac{1}{2}$. These are equivalent fractions.

even

A whole number which can be divided by 2, with nothing left over. It is a multiple of 2. See also *odd*.

F

face

A flat surface on a 3-D shape. See also *edge* and *vertex*.

fraction

Part of a whole.

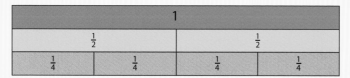

fraction bar

In the fraction $\frac{3}{4}$ the numerator 3 is above the fraction bar and the denominator 4 is below.

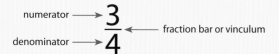

G

gram

Symbol: g. A measure of mass or weight. There are 1000 grams in a kilogram. See also *kilogram*.

greater than

Also called more than. Symbol: >. Used when comparing 2 numbers or measures. 10 is greater than 7, or 10 > 7. See also *less than*.

H

hexagon

A 2-D shape with 6 straight sides.

hour

Symbol: h. A measure of time. See also *minute, second*.

hundred

One hundred, 100, is 10 tens or 1 more than 99.

hundreds

The position in a number where the digit represents hundreds, e.g. in 278 there is a digit 2 in the hundreds place, so there are 2 hundreds.

I

inverse

Addition is the inverse of subtraction, e.g. 16 + 24 = 40, 40 − 24 = 16. Multiplication is the inverse of division, e.g. 4 × 12 = 48, 48 ÷ 12 = 4.

K

kilogram

Symbol: kg. A measure of mass or weight. There are 1000 grams in a kilogram. See also *gram*.

L

less than

Symbol: <. Used when comparing two numbers or measures, e.g. 7 is less than 10, or 7 < 10. See also *greater than*.

line symmetry

A 2-D object or shape has line symmetry if it can be folded into 2 identical halves along a mirror line. Each half is a mirror image of the other.

line of symmetry

litre

Symbol: l . A measure of capacity. 1000 millilitres = 1 litre.

M

mass

Sometimes called weight. How light or heavy something is. Measured in grams and kilograms. See also *gram, kilogram*.

measuring scale

A way of measuring using a line or a dial with equal marks and spacings, like on a ruler.

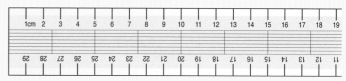

mental calculation

Doing a calculation in your head, but perhaps with jottings.

metre

Symbol: m. A measure of length or height, 100 centimetres = 1 metre.

millilitre

Symbol: ml. A measure of capacity. 1000 millilitres = 1 litre.

minuend

The starting number in a subtraction calculation, e.g. 10 (the minuend) − 3 (the subtrahend) = 7 (the difference). See also *subtrahend* and *difference*.

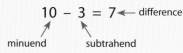

minute

Symbol: min. A measure of time. See also *second* and *hour*.

mixed number

A number with both a whole number part and a fractional part, e.g. $3\frac{1}{2}$.

multiple, multiple of

When you start at zero and count in steps of the same size, those numbers are multiples of that step. So 5, 10, 15, 20, 25 and so on are all multiples of 5.

A multiple is the product of 2 numbers, e.g. the multiples of 3 are 3, 6, 9, 12, 15, 18 and so on.

multiplicand

The number to be multiplied, e.g. in $6 \times 3 = 18$, 6 is the multiplicand. See also *multiplier*.

multiplication table

A list of multiplication facts for a given multiple, often learned by heart.

multiplier

The multiplying number, e.g. in $6 \times 3 = 18$, 3 is the multiplier. See also *multiplicand*.

N

number bonds/pairs

Pairs of numbers with a particular total, e.g. the number bonds for 10 are all pairs of whole numbers, like 2 and 8, which add up to 10.

numeral

The symbol you write to represent a number. We use the arabic numerals 0, 1, 2, 3, 4, 5, 6, 7, 8 and 9.

numerator

The number above the fraction line in a fraction. See also *denominator*.

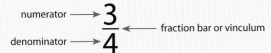

O

octagon

A 2-D shape with 8 straight sides.

odd

A whole number which cannot be divided by 2, there will always be 1 left over. It is not a multiple of 2. See also *even*.

one third, $\frac{1}{3}$

The fraction made when dividing a whole into 3 equal parts.

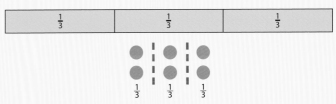

P

pentagon

A 2-D shape with 5 straight sides.

pictogram

A picture to show statistical information. A picture is used to represent 1 or a number of elements.

Walk	😊😊😊😊😊😊😊😊😊😊😊😊
Car	😊😊😊😊😊😊😊
Bicycle	😊😊
Bus	😊😊😊
Taxi	😊😊

Key: 😊 = 1 child

polygon

The general name for 2-D shapes with straight sides. Includes triangle (3 sides), quadrilateral (4 sides), pentagon (5 sides) and so on.

prism

A 3-D shape with 2 identical ends, joined by rectangular faces. The cross-section of a prism is always the same as the ends.

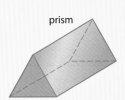

prism

product

The result of multiplying 2 numbers together, e.g. the product of 4 and 3 is $4 \times 3 = 12$.

Q

quadrilateral

A 2-D shape with 4 straight sides. Rectangles, squares and kites are special sorts of quadrilaterals.

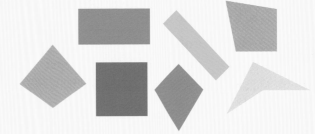

quarter past, quarter to

Quarter past is 15 minutes after (past) the last o'clock time. Quarter to is 45 minutes after the last o'clock time and 15 minutes before the next o'clock time, or quarter of an hour until the next o'clock.

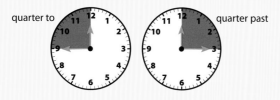

quarter to   quarter past

quotient

The answer to a division calculation, e.g. in $12 \div 6 = 2$, 2 is the quotient. See also *denominator*, *dividend*, *divisor*.

R

rectangular

An object with the shape of a rectangle, which is longer in one direction than the other. Each pair of opposite sides are equal and the angles are all right angles.

right angle

A quarter of a full turn.

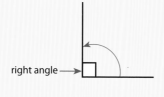

right angle →

row

A list of numbers, shapes or objects across a page, not down, often in a table or an array. See also *column*.

← row

rule

An instruction for carrying out a mathematical operation or continuing a pattern. It can be written using symbols or words. See also *sequence*.

S

second

Symbol: s. A measure of time. See also *hour*, *minute*.

semi-circle

Half of a circle.

sequence

A set of numbers made by following a given rule, e.g. the multiples of 3 are 3, 6, 9 and so on.

single-, 2-, 3-digit numbers

The number of digits in a number, e.g. 3 is a single-digit number, 13 is a 2-digit number and 213 is a 3-digit number.

sorting

Classifying objects, shapes or numbers into groups according to their properties.

straight line

A straight line has no curves or corners and is the shortest distance between 2 points. It can be drawn using a ruler.

subtrahend

The number that is subtracted from the minuend.

sum

An addition of 2 or more numbers or the result of an addition, e.g. augend + addend = sum (or total).

$$3 + 5 = 8$$

augend   addend   sum/total

surface

The face or faces of a 3-D shape. They can be flat like the faces of a cube or curved like the face of a sphere.

symmetry, symmetrical

A figure has line symmetry if it can be folded along a mirror line into 2 identical halves, which are mirror images of each other.

line of symmetry

T

table

An arrangement of numbers or objects in rows and columns See also *array*.

Year 1	Year 2	Year 3	Year 4
2	4	6	3
9	3	4	5
4	2	2	7

tally

A set of marks used for quick and accurate counting. Usually counting in sets of 5 with 4 downward strokes and the 5th stroke is a diagonal line across the 4 downward strokes.

tally chart

A table used to collect information using tally counting.

Travel	Tally	Frequency
Walk	ⅢⅢ Ⅱ	12
Car	ⅢⅢ ⅠⅠⅠⅠ	9
Bicycle	ⅠⅠ	2
Bus	ⅠⅠⅠ	3
Taxi	ⅠⅠ	2

temperature

A measure of hotness. Usually in degrees Celsius, though Centigrade is often still used. Symbol: °C.

tens

The position in a number where the digit represents tens, e.g. in 278 there is a digit 7 in the tens place, so there are 7 tens.

tens boundary

When counting from ones to tens, the tens boundary is crossed.

three-quarters

A fraction of a whole. 3 parts of a whole that has been divided into 4 equal parts.

triangle

A 2-D shape with 3 straight sides.

U

units

The standard measures, e.g. the units of length are metres, centimetres.

V

Venn diagram

A diagram of interlocking circles, used to sort numbers or objects by category.

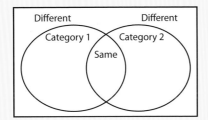

vertex, vertices

The point where 2 or more lines or edges intersect. See also *face*, *edge*.

vertical

Standing up straight.

vinculum

The line that separates the numerator and denominator in a fraction.

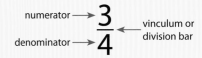

volume

The amount of liquid in a container, e.g. 1 litre of water in a 2-litre bottle. Measured in millilitres and litres. See also *capacity*.